Family Ministry Desk Reference

Family Ministry Desk Reference

Patricia Fosarelli, M.D., D.Min.

Westminster John Knox Press
LOUISVILLE • LONDON

Book design by Sharon Adams
Cover design by Lisa Buckley

First edition
Published by Westminster John Knox Press
Louisville, Kentucky

This book is printed on acid-free paper that meets the American National Standards Institute Z39.48 standard. ∞

PRINTED IN THE UNITED STATES OF AMERICA

03 04 05 06 07 08 09 10 11 12 — 10 9 8 7 6 5 4 3 2 1

Library of Congress Cataloging-in-Publication Data

Fosarelli, Patricia D.
    Family ministry desk reference / Patricia Fosarelli.—1st ed.
      p. cm.
    Includes bibliographical references.
    ISBN 0-664-22668-X (alk. paper)
    1. Church work with families.   2. Family—Religious aspects—Christianity.
  3. Family—Psychological aspects.   I. Title.

BV4438.F67 2004
259′.1—dc21   2003053770

*To all the children and their families
whom I have served in medicine and ministry*

Contents

Introduction

*T*his book grew out of a course that I teach at The Ecumenical Institute of Theology of St. Mary's Seminary & University in Baltimore. Called "Problems of Contemporary Families," the course examines the most common problems facing United States families today. Each problem is examined in terms of the physical, psychological, and spiritual challenges it offers. The responses to each problem are discussed in terms of the practical physical, psychological, and spiritual efforts that either an individual or a congregation can make.

During several years in teaching this course, I tried to find a text that would take the physical, psychological, and spiritual—all three—into account in its discussion of problems; if there was (or is) such a book, it escaped my notice. Hence, this book started as the "writing up" of my research for the class and other pertinent notes. In its present form, it has evolved a great deal from its early stages through its expanded sections on pertinent statistics, recommended readings, and recommended resources for each problem discussed.

In my career as a physician and as a lay minister, I have seen many troubled families, some with multiple problems. Families are composed of living, complex persons whose problems are also complex. Easy solutions never seem to work for very long or at all. Of more importance, in my experience, problems could not be neatly categorized as solely "physical," "psychological," or "spiritual." A physical problem frequently had spiritual ramifications; a spiritual problem had psychological ramifications; and a psychological problem had physical ramifications, and all of these affect not just the individual with the problem, but the entire family. In addition, the complexity of the problems meant that a single-aspect solution might not be enough to address the need created by the problem, either in the individual or in his or her larger family.

In pediatrics, we think of the entire family as our patient. Hence, any response we make to a problem usually must take into account more than what meets the eye, and certainly more than the person with the problem. In other words, we take a more holistic approach to the problem, both in analyzing its effects on a given individual or family and in suggesting appropriate, meaningful responses. Although certain problems are very common these days, each individual and his or her family experience them in a unique fashion, based on their own strengths, weaknesses, and support systems in place.

In most medical practices, the spiritual aspect is not taken fully into account in the analyses and suggested responses to problems. This might be because most physicians and other health care professionals do not always feel comfortable in discussing the spiritual, a topic about which most health professionals learned nothing in medical school or in other professional schools.

Yet in my twenty-six years of pediatrics and my years in lay ministry, spiritual issues are always present, even when the problem is obviously physical (e.g., a broken leg) or psychological (e.g., obsessive-compulsive disorder). For those who have been churched—or at least believe in God—questions such as "Why me?" or "Why is God doing this to me?" surface and demand an answer (or at least some attention), especially as the problem becomes more acute, long-standing, or serious. This might also be true for those who profess no belief in a deity or are unsure of a deity's existence, because "spiritual" takes into account not only one's relationship with God but also with other persons and with all creation.

Although organized health care might be reluctant to broach spiritual issues, ministry should not—*and cannot*—hesitate. But sometimes, before we approach a situation, it would be helpful to have more information about the problems we face in our selves, families, friends, and congregants rather than just our own feelings about the issues. It is good to have some objective information to guide our thinking. That is why this book was written: to provide objective information and insight into pastoral concerns that might be raised by any of the problems discussed, problems that are, unfortunately, all too common in our congregations.

The first four problems covered relate to changes or challenges in family structure, the remaining eleven relate to common difficulties faced by many families. That said, the challenges addressed in this book are these:

- The addition of a family member through birth, adoption, foster care, or elder care
- The loss of a child in pregnancy, at birth, or in infancy
- The loss of a family member through death or divorce
- Single-parent families and stepfamilies
- The sudden loss of possessions, status, pets, employment, or savings

- Moving
- Chronic illness and lack of adequate health insurance or medical care
- Aging
- Substitute care (child care) and latchkey children
- Adolescent sexuality, pregnancy, and parenthood
- School failure, poverty, unemployment, and racism
- Substance abuse, alcoholism, and depression
- Child abuse
- Domestic and societal violence
- The media

Each chapter has primarily the same format: opening vignettes to illustrate the problem; facts and statistics about the problem; physical, emotional, and spiritual challenges posed by the problem; responses to the problem, by individuals or by congregations; resources for more information; references for the statistics given; and an area for users of this book to write the names of resources in their own communities. Although I have tried to include national toll-free numbers for assistance with many of the problems, it is usually best to check which resources are available in one's community by checking the local telephone listings—commercial and governmental.

We are all members of God's family, and so, problems of the families of brothers and sisters affect us all; they are our problems, too. At various times of our lives, we might be called on to minister; at other times, we might be called on to receive ministry from others. So if we share in the problems, we can also share in responding to those with the problems, both as individuals and as congregations. The choice to respond is in our hands.

Chapter 1

Addition of a New Family Member through Birth, Adoption, Foster Care, or Elder Care

Seven-year-old Johnny was miserable. "Why did we have to get a new baby?" he grumbled. "Now I have to share my room with my brother Stevie, and he messes up my stuff all the time. I prayed that God would let me have my room by myself, but God didn't hear me." Meanwhile, Johnny's mother and father were worried about how they would be able to get by without her income. "I didn't realize how much your salary helped us out each month, but I do now," Johnny's father told his wife. "We'll have to cut out extra expenses just to get by."

In another household, Sarah and her husband, Bill, are trying to decide how they can care for Bill's aging father. "We'll just have to put the hospital bed in the living room," said Bill sadly. "Dad can't walk steps." Sarah remarked, "And we thought we would be alone after Tessie went to college!" Bill shook his head, "Such a good man and now so helpless—why does God let these kinds of things happen?"

Physical Challenges

Except in the most affluent families, taking on another family member means finding space for her. Whereas the previously childless couple had the entire apartment to themselves, with the birth of their first child they will now have less room. In the case of a couple with limited space and one child already, that child might have to surrender his own room to give the new baby a place to sleep. Depending on the age of the child, that adjustment may be easy or very difficult. When a family takes in an elderly relative, even more physical

4

General Comments and Facts to Consider

When discussing problems of contemporary families, it might seem odd to categorize the addition of a new member as a "problem." For most families, the birth of a baby or the adoption of a child is a much-desired event. For other families, however, the birth of a baby is not desired, and even the longed-for adoption turns out to be not what the new parents expected. Even in the best of situations, the addition of a new family member will necessitate changes in living arrangements and style of living. This chapter describes some of the physical, emotional, and spiritual changes that the addition of a new family member entails.

1. Each year in this country, there are four million births. Of these, approximately 5,000 infants have heart malformations; 3,300 have cleft lip/palate; 1,600 have Down's syndrome; and 650 have spina bifida or meningocele (National Center for Health Statistics). Of the four million births, 7.4 percent are low birth weight (<2500 grams) and an additional 1.4 percent are very low birth weight (<1500 grams). Women most likely to have a low birth weight infant are those less than twenty years of age and those greater than forty years. Children who are born with low birth weight are at risk for medical problems and future learning problems.

2. Only about 2 percent of the child population in the United States is adopted. In recent times, many children have been adopted from Romania and other countries in the former Soviet bloc, as well as from China. In 1995, nearly 10,000 international adoptees were brought into the United States (Barnett 29), often at great expense to the adoptive parents. When children are adopted from countries whose economic standards are poor by U.S. standards, there is a good chance that these children are malnourished and might not have received proper preventive health care (such as immunizations) or medical care for conditions that they have. Regardless of country of origin, poor nutrition early in life can play a role in the appropriate development of the brain, neurologic system, and other organs of the body.

3. The exact number of children in foster care is not known because of poor record keeping and a constant process of entry, exit, and reentry. On any given day, there might be approximately 500,000 children younger than nineteen years of age in foster care in the United States. Minorities are overrepresented. Although girls and boys are equally represented in the system, their reasons for being in foster care differ. Girls are more likely to have been sexually abused, whereas boys are more likely to have been physically abused or physically, cognitively, or emotionally impaired. Adolescents comprise over half of the children in foster care. Many children in foster care are "unadoptable" because of their older age, minority status, or emotional problems. Twenty to thirty percent of children who were returned to their biologic families reenter the foster care system over time. Although 50 percent of children return to their families within thirty days of placement, 25 percent remain in foster care for over two years. Contrary to popular belief, most foster parents assume care for difficult children out of a sense of regard for the children's welfare and not for financial remuneration; many of them will actually incur significant out-of-pocket expenses for the children in their care (Schor 209–10).

4. A 1992 national survey found that nearly 33 percent of adults in the United States aged 55 and older serve as caregivers of family, friends, or neighbors; moreover, the bulk of the care is provided by women rather than men (Bronfenbrenner 226).

adjustments must be made, because frequently the relative will have his own property. If the relative is also ill, bulky medical equipment perhaps must be at hand.

Loss of personal time and privacy becomes an issue. When a new person enters a family, whether she is an infant or an older person, someone must yield time to care for her, and in this process a degree of independence and a measure of privacy are lost. Depending on the needs of the new family member and the temperament of the primary caregiver, this loss of time and privacy might be much more than a minor inconvenience. For example, the addition of a new baby brings a constant flow of tasks that must be done, even when the baby is sleeping. The addition of an ill, older relative brings its own set of tasks that must be performed in a timely fashion to ensure that his days are as comfortable as possible.

For the couple who had only their own needs to consider, this loss affects them as a couple and individually. Time together—for physical, sexual, and emotional intimacy—might be at a premium. In the case of the addition of a small infant to the family, sleep time will also be compromised when the baby requires feeding throughout the night. This will cause fatigue and stress for the parent primarily responsible for the child's care at night. It will also cause stress for the parent who doesn't have to manage those needs, especially if he must work during the day. A crying or fussy baby will preclude a hoped-for night of uninterrupted sleep.

The addition of a family member might also necessitate a tightening of the family finances. After all, there is another person to clothe and feed, to say nothing of extraordinary needs such as medications, special equipment, transportation needs, and so on. The addition of a new child in the family requires parents to begin to save money for the child's education, even if it is many years in the future. For infants and small children, the cost of formula and diapers is an expense that is higher than most parents originally anticipate. The drain on finances might require one parent (usually the father) to take on another job to make ends meet. This further limits the time that the couple has with each other and can lead to even more stress in their relationship.

Finally, the amount of time required by individuals with special needs should not be underestimated. Infants with special needs might require tube feedings to increase their caloric intake or frequent suctioning of their airway to help them breathe more easily. An older person who is ill might require special procedures or medication administration at fixed times of the day. An adopted child or foster child might require increased help with homework and time for just "being together" with a caring adult.

Emotional Challenges

The addition of a new family member can be a time of great rejoicing, but it can also be a time of great stress. If the new infant or adopted/foster child is less than what the parents expected (i.e., if there are physical limitations or emotional challenges), the parents might feel anger or resentment. *This is so even when they love the child.* The sense of disappointment that comes with not getting the child of their hopes and dreams must be taken seriously. If this is a child of their own biological making, they might be embarrassed that they produced a less-than-perfect child and might avoid social contacts. If this is a child whom they have chosen through adoption or foster placement, they might second-guess themselves, wondering if they really made the correct decision.

In such circumstances, there is always an amount of grieving that must occur. This is not always recognized by relatives and friends. Parents mourn the loss of their dream and mourn the loss of the life that they once knew. They wonder if life will ever be "normal" again in the way they used to understand normalcy.

Even when a child is entirely normal, many parents grieve the loss of their independence and individual time with each other. The young infant can be very demanding because she is so helpless. Her demands might take up most of the day. Parents, in their exhaustion, may have little time left over for each other or other children. An especially demanding infant might require even more time investment, leaving parents increasingly fatigued and frustrated.

Maternal depression after the birth of a child is not uncommon and stems from the mismatch between a mother's dreams and reality. A father who feels that he has no real role in the care of a young infant may be frustrated by the amount of time that the mother must devote to the infant, time that once was reserved for him. Tempers may flare. In other situations, a new father may work longer hours just to stay away from home. Siblings also might resent the amount of time that their parents must devote to the new infant, because they now receive proportionately less time themselves. Although mild sibling rivalry is entirely normal, in extreme instances the older siblings may try to seriously hurt a new baby.

The addition of an older adopted child or a foster child can create even more problems. When such children are older, much of their personality and temperament may already be in place, making adjustment a two-way street with their new parents. In addition, depending on how badly they had been abused or neglected, these children may have a number of psychological problems that have nothing to do with their new family, but with which the new family will have to cope. If there are older siblings in the family, acquiring a new brother or sister with behavior problems may not be what they had in mind when they were told that they would be getting a new sibling. Sibling rivalry is common. Also, the newly adopted child or the foster child might respond to his new siblings with maladaptive behaviors learned in a previous environment.

The addition of an older relative into a household will change that family's life greatly. The older person definitely has her own needs, wants, and coping mechanisms, based on a lifetime of experiences. In addition, if she is ill, these needs and desires might be heightened, and coping mechanisms might be stretched to the limit. A good deal of patience is needed from all concerned. Because an ill relative might need more rest and quiet, parents might curtail their children's normal, active behavior indoors; this might cause the children to resent the older person, even though they truly love her. In addition, if the parent must devote a great deal of time to care for the older relative, a child might also resent the loss of parental time. The caring parent, the member of the "in-between generation," might feel squeezed to the limit by the many responsibilities for both the younger and older generations; she might feel that she cannot do an adequate job for anyone. This can lead to frustration, anger, hostility, burnout, and depression.

Spiritual Challenges

An addition of another family member might not seem, on the surface, to engender much of a spiritual crisis; yet even with the addition of a completely healthy and wanted child, parents might occasionally question if this was really the right time. Certainly, parents will wonder what kind of person this new child will become.

If the newborn is born prematurely, ill, or with congenital anomalies, parents may well ask themselves, "Why? Why did God permit us to have such a child? Is God angry at us? Are we being punished for some reason?" Guilt may be the overarching spiritual response, especially if the parents believe that they are being punished for their own indiscretions, past or present. In addition, if the baby suffers because of needed medical procedures, parents may feel even more guilt, as if they themselves caused their infant such pain. Such parents may have great difficulty trusting that God will give them the resources necessary to live each day to its fullest.

Similarly, there are spiritual crises associated with adopting a child or taking in a foster child. Parents may wonder if and why God led them to make such a decision, especially if the child proves to be difficult emotionally or medically. Moreover, their faith in God may be shaken if the child rejects them (because of his previous experiences), especially if they believed that their reception of this child was God's will. In such cases, parents might fantasize "returning" the child and "getting back to normal." These feelings may lead to enormous guilt and shame.

Taking in an older relative has its own set of spiritual crises as well. Questions about "Why us?" abound. "Why my father? Why our family? Why this time? How are we going to cope?" In addition, if the relative is very ill, severely incapacitated, or dying, issues of mortality need to be faced squarely. It is uncomfortable to live with someone who is a daily reminder of one's mortality. When that person also makes demands on the caregiver's time, energy, and resources, it is easy to understand how questions arise about God's role in this situation. For example, "Dad lived such a good life; why is he suffering so now?" "We've always been so active in church; why is this happening to our family?" These questions will be even more anguished if end-of-life decisions need to be made, especially if the older person is not capable of participating fully in their crafting.

Individual Responses

Individual responses to a family who has assumed care for another member may be as simple as offering to babysit other children, to carpool children to school or after-school activities, or to invite children over to one's house to play. This gives the new mother or the person who has a new responsibility to care for an ill relative a chance to get some breathing room, or a chance to devote some time to the new member without the other children present.

If the family in need so desires, a helping individual may be able to run some errands, cook, or shop for them. Becoming a loving presence might mean simply listening when the caregiver feels that he or she cannot go on. Or it might mean staying with the new baby, child, or ill relative while the caregiver gets some time away from the home, either alone or with the spouse. It certainly includes praying for the entire family. It does not, however, include taking sides in family disagreements or offering unsolicited advice.

The individual who wants to help can also learn about resources in the community that could help the stressed family and share this information with the family *and* the pastoral staff of the congregation, who might be unaware of this information and would benefit from knowing of available community services.

Congregational Responses

In addition to making a visit to the family experiencing a crisis, the pastor can urge congregants to organize a ministry of visitation to such families, offering periods of respite from the hard work of caring for a challenging new member. The pastor or members of the pastoral team can look for educational resources (printed materials as well as speakers) to facilitate the development of this type of ministry. Perhaps education about a particular problem is needed—children with birth defects, elderly stroke victims, adoptees from foreign countries, and so forth—depending on the need in a particular congregation, especially if more than one family in the congregation is affected by the same circumstance.

The pastor can encourage prayers for families with new members at each week's liturgy and can preach about the need to be with families in their good times and more stressful ones, emphasizing the ministry of simple presence. Indeed, a ministry of *presence* might be far preferable to a ministry of *presents*. The simple ways that such a ministry can occur both on an individual level and a congregational one can be highlighted, especially when the Scripture readings for the day underscore hospitality. The pastor can remind congregants that the reason that Jesus was so appealing to ordinary people was that he was willing to be present with them both in their good times and in their bad times. Today's Christians are called to do no less.

Finally, the congregation can welcome new children—adoptees and foster children—publicly at worship and socially afterward. Everybody likes a good party, and it is good for the community to celebrate not only the newly baptized infants but all new children. If the new child has been adopted from a foreign country, the entire congregation (but especially the children) can be given some information about the customs of his or her native country. The congregation can also celebrate adults newly in their midst. Although such a celebration may not be welcomed by some adults, others will embrace it as a chance to get to know people in their new faith community. Such hospitality for the stranger is one way a congregation more perfectly mirrors Christ's actions and honors his enduring presence.

REFERENCES

Barnett, E., and Miller, L. "International Adoption: The Pediatrician's Role." *Contemporary Pediatrics* (August 1996), 13:29–46.

Bronfenbrenner, U., McClelland, P., Wethington, E., et al. *The State of Americans*. New York: The Free Press, 1996.

Schor, E. "Foster Care." *Pediatrics in Review* (1989), 10:209–16.

STATISTICS

National Center for Health Statistics

   www.cdc.gov/nchs/fastats/births.htm
   www.cdc.gov/nchs/fastats/bdefects.htm
   www.calib.com/nccanch/pubs/factsheets/foster.cfm
   www.acf.hhs.gov/programs/cb/publications/afcars/report7.htm

FOR MORE INFORMATION

See local telephone listings under "adoption," "Catholic Charities," "foster care" (under "social services"), "elder care," "adult day-care services," and "support groups."

LOCAL RESOURCES

_____

_____

_____

_____

_____

Chapter 2

Death in Pregnancy and Infancy

*T*wo months after her miscarriage, Anne remains in mourning. "No one understands what I am going through," Anne says to her husband, Bill. "I am so sick of people acting like it was no big deal that I miscarried. When they say things like, 'You're young; you can always get pregnant again,' or 'You have one healthy child; why aren't you satisfied?' I feel like screaming! I lost my *baby!* Even though she was never born, she was alive—she moved inside of me. I had dreams for her. She was our child. And the worst part is that just because she was never *born*, we couldn't even have a funeral for her. It's like she never existed." Bill just looks at Anne, not knowing what to say.

It was Easter Sunday, the day celebrating new life, when Tammy and Lee found their three-month-old son lifeless in his crib. He had been fine just a couple hours earlier when Tammy fed him and dressed him up for church. But, when Lee went in to get him, he was not breathing. Nothing could save him. Although the autopsy said it was SIDS (Sudden Infant Death Syndrome) and not Tammy and Lee's fault that he died, they blamed themselves and each other for his death. Maybe Tammy shouldn't have fed him so much; maybe Lee should have checked on him sooner. Worst of all, their families are starting to take sides and speculating on whose fault his death was.

Physical Challenges

A loss during pregnancy affects women in different ways; some women's bodies adjust rapidly to their nonpregnant state, whereas other women find their bodies adjust much more slowly. Physical intimacy and sexual relations

General Comments and Facts to Consider

The loss of a child *at any age* is devastating. This is true for a loss during pregnancy as well—which many people seem to forget. A child is the visible sign of a couple's love for each other; a child is their future. When a child dies, even before birth, hopes and dreams die too. If a couple struggled to become pregnant, the loss is even more traumatic. They wonder if they will ever be able to get pregnant again. They wonder if they are at fault for their inability to have a child or at fault for their child's death.

The loss of an infant is also devastating to older children in the family who might have been overjoyed at the prospect of having a baby sister or brother. If older children knew that their mother was pregnant, they will also grieve a loss in pregnancy or at the time of birth. It is always a mistake to think that children are too young to notice or to care about such things.

1. For every 1,000 pregnancies, seven end before 28 weeks of gestation and an additional three after 28 weeks. For every 1,000 live births, over seven children die before they are 28 days of age (National Vital Statistics System).

2. Leading causes of infant death are congenital anomalies, pre-term/low birth weight, SIDS, complications related to pregnancy, and respiratory disease (National Center for Health Statistics).

between wife and husband might be changed or nonexistent for weeks or months following the loss.

An additional physical challenge is the home environment. When they find out that they are going to have a baby, most couples begin to buy things for the baby and decorate what will be the baby's room. A loss during pregnancy brings such preparations to a halt. In fact, the mere presence of "the baby's room" or infant clothes, furniture, or toys is a constant reminder of the parents' loss.

The death of an infant is even more wrenching in this regard because parents *remember* their baby in the crib, wearing the outfits, or playing with the toys. The normal sounds of an infant—crying, cooing, coughing, sneezing—are no more but continue to resonate in their memories. Parents might want to leave the room exactly the way it was on the day of the baby's death, or they might want to discard or give away everything that belonged to their child in an effort to eradicate the memories and the pain.

If there are other children in the home, other physical challenges will be present. If an older child had his belongings moved in preparation to share a room with a new baby, the older child might have to rearrange these belongings. If a child shared a room with an infant sibling who died, she might have to readjust to having a room for herself again, as the baby's belongings are moved out. In addition, the sibling will also miss the company and physical intimacy—the sights, sounds, and *fun*—of having someone so near. Young children tend to talk to their infant siblings, and the surviving child might miss those "conversations" a great deal, missing his sibling's coos, cries, or giggles. This is especially true in the middle of the night when the room is dark and just a bit scary.

Emotional Challenges

When parents lose a child, whether born or unborn, they feel as if they have lost part of themselves. And, of course, that is true. Mention has already been made of their grief over their loss. Parents might express this grief in vastly different ways, perhaps leading one parent to accuse the other of hysteria, whereas the second parent accuses the first of indifference. One parent might need to talk about the baby, whereas the other parent prefers to "move on" and not think about the painful past. One parent might need to be held, whereas the other parent stiffens at any touch. Some grieving parents immerse themselves in work or other activities away from home to ease their pain; a parent left at home might feel abandoned and unsupported. Other parents attempt to escape their grief through use of alcohol, substance abuse, or sexual activity outside of the marriage. When the coping strategies of the two parents are radically different, a distance might develop between them that precludes emotional and physical intimacy.

When a child dies, many individuals feel the need to assign blame; in their minds, the death must have been *someone's* fault. A husband might blame his wife for not taking better care of herself during pregnancy; a wife might blame her husband for being too rough during sexual intercourse or wanting sex too often. The father of an infant might blame the mother for feeding the baby too much, whereas the mother might blame the father for disregarding the baby's cries. Naturally, each parent might blame him- or herself, silently or openly. Blaming, like different styles of mourning and coping, might lead to arguments between the parents and difficulties in their marital relationship.

Grandparents and other family members can also assign blame and take sides, further splitting the parents. At a time when parents really *need* everyone's support, partisan behavior by family members only increases the stress and makes it more likely that difficulties will develop. This is especially likely if relationships between the couple and the respective in-laws were troubled *before* the loss of the child.

The problem of what to do with the belongings of the baby is also fraught with emotion and tension. Some persons believe that rooms should be left just "as is" as a tribute to the one who died. Others rush to discard anything that even hints of the deceased. Naturally, a middle ground is the best position, but in such a highly emotional time, it is very difficult not to lean toward one extreme or the other in the immediate period after the death. The belongings of the deceased are so personal and are a constant reminder of the life that once was, born or unborn.

Other children in the family also present an emotional challenge for parents. At a time when parents need more time to themselves and for each other, children might demand more time because they are frightened by their parents' sadness, anger, or absence. Hence, children might become demanding, whiny, clingy, fussy; they might also revert to behaviors more characteristic of themselves at a younger age, or they might demonstrate temper tantrums. Such children are trying to draw some parental attention to themselves at a time when it seems, to them, that parental attention is elsewhere. Their sleep, appetite, and activity patterns might also be disrupted, just as their parents' might be. Everyone's life has been disrupted; everyone's nerves might be on edge.

Children also have concerns of their own. If they had resisted a new baby in the family, were jealous of the baby, or said or did things to hurt the baby, they might experience a great deal of guilt, as if their actions, words, or feelings caused the death. They might fear their "power." On the other hand, they might fear their absolute powerlessness (and that of their parents) because no one in the family was able to save the baby. If they get sick or injured, will someone be able to save them? Will they be the next to die? Will their parents die? What will happen to them if their parents die? These fears are all the more marked if parents are arguing a great deal, are absent from the home more than usual, or are handling their grief poorly (e.g., lack of personal hygiene, alcohol or substance abuse, physical or verbal abuse between the spouses or directed at the children).

Siblings might also just *miss* their baby brother or sister because they loved him or shared a room with her. Thus they might have their own ways of grieving, and these might not be those of adults. Young children might grieve through tears and sadness, but they might also grieve by acting out—fighting, yelling, arguing, sassing, and the like. They might also act nonchalantly about the loss, as if it were no big deal.

Spiritual Challenges

"Why is God doing this to us?" is a frequent question asked by parents who have lost an infant. After such a loss, parents might doubt God's love, fairness, or even existence. They might not want to pray, or they might openly express anger toward God and things or persons associated with God, such as clergy, chaplains, church, prayers, or hymns. Some parents believe that their infant died because God was punishing them for some real or imagined transgression; frequently, the transgression is related to sexual thoughts, feelings, words, or actions. For example, a woman who had a sexually transmitted disease during her wilder college years might attribute her miscarriage to punishment for her sexual promiscuity. A man who pressured his former girlfriend to obtain an abortion might feel that God is "getting even" with him. Both men and women can attribute loss during pregnancy, at birth, or after birth to marital indiscretions. Sometimes spouses know about these affairs, but sometimes they do not. In the latter case, the current time is usually not the optimal time to disclose them when the spouse is already upset about the loss.

Parents can also believe that God is "testing" them for some reason or that God doesn't care about them. Beliefs like this can lead to a very negative impression of God—one of a deity who hurts small infants in order to deal with adults. This impression is especially likely if the parents are feeling guilty about their behavior and if the infant suffered a great deal before he or she died.

Children can pick up negative impressions about God from their parents or other relatives. This can be very frightening to children who might already believe that God is punishing *them* for their mean thoughts, words, or actions, which had been directed toward their (now deceased) sibling. When adults make such comments around young children as "God's will *will* be done" or "What did you expect—do you think that God was going to let you get away with your actions?" even if such comments are addressed toward adults, children might fully internalize them.

When an infant has died, there are some comments about God that are not at all helpful to say to children. For example, when a five-year-old asked why his baby sister died, a relative said, "God needed another angel in heaven." Such a comment might lead a child to wonder why *he* wasn't picked to be an angel. Isn't he good enough? Or he might wonder that if God made everything that we see, why did God need to take his baby sister? Couldn't God have just made another angel? Or he might worry that if God needs another angel in the future, God will come after *him*. Although people make such comments to help a child, in the end, such a comment backfires because it is not based on sound theology, sound child developmental theory, or good pastoral care.

Children might also be disappointed or angry if they prayed for their infant sibling to get better and that didn't occur. They might worry that God didn't hear the prayer or worse yet, God doesn't care or is angry at the child. Alternatively, some children have prayed for their new baby sister or brother to go away. When death occurs, such children are miserable, fearful that their prayers have too much power. They might stop praying altogether because they are so frightened of this "power."

Individual Responses

Individuals should not ignore the fact that someone has experienced a loss—whether in pregnancy, at the time of birth, or sometime after birth. This is especially true for losses during pregnancy. Parents need to know that the life that they brought into being *is* important and is recognized by others. Not knowing what to say is not an excuse to say nothing.

One should avoid saying things like, "You're young; you can have another baby," or "It's all for the better." Such comments are not comforting at the time of the loss. Even though many such comments may be offered to make people feel better, they are often interpreted as insensitive and may make people feel worse because the comments devalue the loss and fail to take it seriously. Loss during pregnancy *is* a real loss; it is the loss of a living being and the loss of a dream. How can the death of a treasured child be "for the better"? How does having "another baby" replace the one who has died? Suppose the infant had been murdered; would one then be tempted to say, "It's all for the better"? Similarly, using clichés such as "God needed another little angel, and that's why he took Tommy" does not necessarily comfort adults and might cause confusion in the one hearing the comment.

The most simple thing to say is, "I'm sorry for your loss." This can be said to either the woman or the man experiencing the loss. The statement does not need to be embellished. It is always a mistake to talk about one's own experience of loss unless one *knows for certain* that such sharing of information would be helpful. This means that one knows the people experiencing the loss very well or that the people have asked about the speaker's own loss. Making judgments or giving opinions about why the loss happened is unacceptable. Equally unacceptable is to ask a string of questions, such as "Did the doctors say why it happened?" "Had you been eating right?" "This happened to my daughter and the doctor said she was anemic; are you anemic?" Such questions are intrusive because they can be interpreted as nosy or judgmental.

Similarly, if the loss is that of an infant, comments such as "What did the autopsy show?" "Had you taken him to the doctor because of his cold?" "You fed him and then an hour later he had died? Didn't you notice anything wrong with him while you were feeding him?" imply that the parent is somehow responsible for the death because of something he or she did or didn't do. Parents blame themselves enough without inquirers contributing to that blame.

One *can* ask how the parent(s) and other children in the family are doing. Adults frequently ask about other adults but less frequently ask about children, yet children are feeling the loss also and deserve concern and care.

As with every problem covered in this book, asking what someone needs is better than making assumptions about what he or she needs, based on one's own needs or desires. A simple "I'd like to help if I could. Is there anything that I can do for you or your family?" expresses one's concern but still permits the person experiencing the loss to decline the offer gracefully or to state what *really* would be the most helpful to do. If a request is made by the person experiencing the loss, a promise to honor it should not be made unless one has every intention of following through. In such a difficult time, to have one's friends or acquaintances let one down is extraordinarily disappointing, especially if they asked what they could do in the first place but subsequently failed to honor their own commitment.

In addition, one can—and *should*—keep those who have lost an infant before, during, or after birth in their prayers, offer to be a safe person with whom they can share their feelings, and offer moral support in any ways that one can.

Congregational Responses

Most congregations will have a prayer list for those who are ill or for those who have died. Many individuals who have lost a child during pregnancy might also appreciate being on this list, but their desires about this should be sought prior to publishing their names or saying their names aloud during a worship service. Some people need their privacy at the time of grief.

If an infant had been ill for a long time before his or her death (e.g., with extreme prematurity, congenital disorder or malformation, heart disease, etc.), the congregation has probably already been praying for him or her, but, again, it is best to determine parental wishes about the publishing or saying aloud of a child's name, even if it seems that no harm could be done.

It is important to keep the *family* of the deceased infant in the minds and hearts of fellow congregants rather than just the deceased infant, as is the practice in some churches. The family includes *any and all* relatives who might have been affected by an infant's death, such as siblings, grandparents, and so on. Unfortunately, grandparents are often forgotten at times of loss when so much attention is focused on the parents.

If there are a sufficient number of parents who have lost children, a congregation might consider a bereavement ministry or a support group of grieving parents; persons who have lost children during pregnancy would also be included in such a group. Perhaps someone from the congregation with expertise in this area could act as facilitator, and speakers could be brought in for presentations, not only to the group but also, at least occasionally, for the benefit of the entire congregation as well. Such a step could raise the awareness and sensitivity of all involved. If there are very few persons who have lost an infant in the congregation, perhaps the pastoral staff could refer individuals experiencing such loss to groups or resources available in the local community. Pastoral staff should be aware of the community resources for parents who have lost infants (e.g., Compassionate Friends) and should have contact information in order to be able to refer those in need of assistance with their grief.

A congregation could consider whether it should conduct an annual service for all persons who have lost children—before, during, or after birth. Such a service demonstrates a congregation's loving concern for *all* its members. This type of service also might help bring closure to those who have lost a child during pregnancy and who never had an opportunity for a funeral to say good-bye. It is at such trying times as the loss of an infant that a congregation can declare their Christian care, ministry, and hospitality in important ways— ways that might spell the difference between a family's ability to heal from the pain of the loss and a family's inability to come to closure.

Alternatively, some congregations have a worship service for persons who have experienced loss during pregnancy. After all, infants and children have funeral services, but what do fetuses receive? Of even more importance, what do their parents and siblings receive in the way of Christian comfort? Appropriate readings can be selected; perhaps family members can take part in the service. Such a service may make the difference between a family who thinks their faith has failed them in their time of need and another family who feels completely supported by their pastor and fellow congregants. Such is the difference between a nominally Christian community and a truly Christian one.

STATISTICS
National Vital Statistics System
   www.cdc.gov/nchs/fastats/infmort.htm

FOR MORE INFORMATION
Check local telephone listings under "Compassionate Friends," "support groups," "funeral directors," and "bereavement services." Funeral directors frequently have useful printed information on grief, coping, and so forth.

LOCAL RESOURCES

_____

_____

_____

_____

_____

Chapter 3

Loss of a Family Member
through Death or Divorce

*M*arsha just sits at her window and cries every evening when six o'clock comes around, for that is the time when her husband Tom used to arrive home from work. But, no longer. Tom died three months ago after a heart attack. Marsha still can't believe it. "I can't believe I'm going to be this miserable for the rest of my life," she cries. "Some days it gets so bad that I just want to die. I'm so lonely in this big house by myself. Why did God take my Tom?"

Fourteen-year-old Tim is angry and embarrassed. "Why did I get such loser parents?" he moans. "It's just my luck to get a father who likes his work more than his family and a mother who likes to drink. And now, they don't even want to live in the same house. I'll never get married—it's not worth the hassle." When asked if he still attends church, Tim asks, "Why should I? God could have made my folks stay together if He had wanted to. So, if He doesn't have time for me, I don't want Him."

Physical Challenges

The family experiencing the dying of one of its members must become accustomed to the marked changes in him. Loss of weight, diminished energy, apathy, irritability, and sadness are frequent characteristics of one who is dying slowly from a chronic condition. It is difficult for other family members to see their loved one becoming more ill. Young children simply do not understand, for example, why their father can no longer play ball with them, why their mother cannot take them to the park, or why their brother only wants to sleep. In addition, children are often frightened by the dying person's appearance.

Facts to Consider

1. There are two million deaths in the United States annually; the top five causes of death are heart disease, cancer, stroke, lung disease, and accidents. Suicides account for approximately 30,000 deaths each year (National Center for Health Statistics).

2. Approximately 5 percent of children under fifteen years of age experience the death of one or both parents (Green 84), creating an enormous number of grieving families.

3. There are over 1.1 million divorces each year (National Center for Health Statistics). More than one million U.S. children are affected by divorce each year (Wallerstein 197).

4. Approximately 43 percent of first marriages end in separation or divorce within fifteen years, but this varies by age: 59 percent of marriages of brides under eighteen years of age ended in divorce compared with 36 percent of those married at age 20 or over (National Center for Health Statistics).

5. More than 50 percent of first marriages end in divorce before the child reaches eighteen years of age; 85 percent of parents who divorce remarry, and 40 percent of these new unions also end in divorce (Dell 57). Perhaps as many as 50 percent of divorced persons remarry within five years, but informal live-in arrangements are even more common (Emery 306). By age 30, about half of U.S. women have cohabited outside of marriage. The likelihood of cohabitation breaking up is twice as high as a marriage (National Center for Health Statistics). This high incidence of divorce and subsequent "living together" creates a staggering number of children who are grieving over the loss of the families they once knew.

6. By 1990, 30 percent of all U.S. children lived in a household in which the adults were divorced or remarried (Dell 57).

The loss of a parent, whether by divorce or death, frequently necessitates a change in living arrangements for the family. At the same time that the family must deal with its grief, new financial constraints surface. Loss of income may be drastic or more modest. For example, only essential clothing, food, and supplies might be affordable, or chances to eat out or to enjoy recreation that costs money may be just a memory of happier times, only rarely permitted after the loss.

The physical loss of a parent leaves a great void in the family, especially when the items that belong to that individual are seen unused or lying vacant. It is no easier when a child dies, for the parents and other siblings are painfully reminded of the deceased child by his toys and clothing. Often, when a family member dies, the family leaves her room "just as it was" on the day of death.

A parent who has lost a spouse through death or divorce misses the intimacy that once existed between them. A surviving parent mourns the loss of an active sexual life, and this may have begun even before the spouse with a terminal condition died. But more than intercourse, the spouse left alone misses the physical intimacy of hugs, shared laughter or tears, or activities in which they once took part as a couple.

Physical signs and symptoms of grief are numerous. There might be much crying, and frank depression is common. Children may manifest their depression by tearfulness or acting-out behaviors, such as aggressiveness, fighting, or name calling. Inattention may also be a sign of depression. Schoolwork may suffer, and relationships with friends may deteriorate. Many unaffected children do not know how to relate to peers whose parents have died or have gotten a divorce, so they may attempt to shun them.

Emotional Challenges

The loss of a significant family member causes grief for those who loved the person. Whether this loss is due to death or to divorce, grieving is expected and can be profound. If the dying process had been prolonged over months, family members continue the grieving that began long before the death as they watched the diminution of their loved one's vitality. When the death was sudden, grief is initially intermingled with shock. As noted above, grief may take many forms, especially in children. Life is never going to be what it once was. Family members long for the "good old days," even though they may not have been so good when carefully considered.

When loss is due to divorce, the child may idealize the absent parent. This places the remaining parent at a great disadvantage in terms of securing the child's cooperation in household tasks or schoolwork, especially if the absent parent was the more lenient of the two. The child may forget the actions of the noncustodial parent that precipitated the divorce, and instead dream of the time when he can live with that parent. In addition, the child may pray or wish that the parents get back together. The parent who is left with the children experiences the loss of not having a partner with whom to share the everyday joys and trials of parenthood.

Guilt is also a major component of the reaction to loss. Depending on the child's age, it is easy for a child to believe that she caused the marital breakup ("If only I had been better, Daddy wouldn't have left.") or even the death of a parent. Many a child has argued with a parent only to have that parent die suddenly and unexpectedly. The resulting guilt is enormous, especially if the child had said, "I wish you were dead" during the course of the argument. Naturally, the same dynamics hold for parents if the situation is reversed. In the case of a sibling who dies, the remaining children may be consumed with guilt over imagined and real wrongs delivered to the now deceased child, such as being mean, tattling, refusing to play with or help him, and so on. Sadness may completely overwhelm the remaining children. Some children cope by taking care of their parents, some by crying, others by acting out, and still others by becoming vulnerable children themselves. Changes in eating, sleeping, cleanliness, schoolwork, and peer relationships are common. With the stress inherent in the loss of any family member, the dynamics of the entire family may be turned askew, as members of the family argue, accuse each other of failing to love the departed family member sufficiently, or take sides against other family members.

Both children and adults experience anger with the loss of a loved one, whether by death or by divorce. Understandably, children may have a great deal of anger toward parents who divorce; a parent may have a great degree of shame and anger toward the other parent if the divorce was precipitated by that parent's substance abuse or adultery. The remaining parent may wonder, "Wasn't I good enough? Was I so lacking that she had to turn to drugs?" "What was wrong with me that he had to find another woman?" In the midst of adultery, the wronged partner's self-esteem suffers enormously.

Adults and children may also be angry toward a family member who has died. Obviously, this is irrational unless the loved one took his own life, but emotions frequently are irrational. "Why did he leave us?" "If she loved us, why did she continue to smoke?" If the death was particularly prolonged and agonizing, as from a malignancy or AIDS, both children and adults can be scarred by the experience.

This is especially true of AIDS, because we, as a society, have still not come to terms with the fact that AIDS is an infection caused by a virus that cannot be cured. Instead, a prevalent belief is that AIDS is "different"; it is a result of moral depravity, and, hence, is deserved by its victims. Does any person, especially a child, really deserve to die a prolonged, excruciating death? Like most plagues throughout history, the AIDS epidemic has taken on moral overtones that just do not make sense when victims are considered as individuals. In our society, there is still shame in having AIDS or in being related to someone who has AIDS, and there is great social stigma attached to the entire family. For such reasons, families that have members with AIDS reveal their situations to very few persons because they are afraid of the social or economic repercussions if the "wrong" people knew.

Although Kübler-Ross originally described emotional stages experienced by the dying (and their families), the stages really apply to nearly every kind of loss. It is instructive to review the stages here. The first stage is marked by denial ("It can't be true"; "The tests were wrong"; "She didn't really mean that she would leave"), whereas the primary coping strategy of the second stage is anger toward others—doctors, relatives, manufacturers of cigarettes, and so forth. The third stage is marked by active bargaining ("If I get better, I'll never smoke again"; "If I get better, I'll live a better life from now on"; "If he comes back, I'll never argue with him again"), whereas the fourth stage is marked by sadness that the situation *is* grim, and, short of a miracle, one's condition is not going to get better. In the fifth stage, the person comes to accept his dying (or, in the case of other losses, one accepts one's situation). Obviously, the relatives and friends of a dying person pass through these stages as well.

Although these stages are useful to understand better the emotional dynamics of dying, one should not assume that these stages are discrete and unrepeatable—that is, traversed once and never entered again. In reality, persons experiencing loss pass in and out of these stages many times; some stages coexist with others. At times, some people skip certain stages altogether, and some people die without ever coming to acceptance. Neither do their relatives and friends, especially when a death is sudden. Again, these dynamics are true not only of the dying and those close to them, but also of adults and children experiencing other types of losses.

Especially problematic are situations in which the deceased has died by suicide, drug overdose, or motor-vehicle injury because of alcohol consumption. Questions arise constantly, "How did we miss her pain?" "What could we have done differently?" "Why didn't we insist on his getting help for his drinking problem?" "Why did we let her drive?" "What did we do to make him give up?" "Why didn't we tell her that we loved her more often?" Family members will blame themselves and each other as they try to make sense of the senseless. The resulting stress can tear a family apart.

Spiritual Challenges

The problems presented in this book lead one to ask God "Why?" and this problem is no exception. "Why did God let my little sister die?" "Why did God let my folks break up?" "Why did God take my brother and not me?" "Why did God let my mother drink and drive?" Such questions are not easily answered, and facile responses are useless. Children may cry out to God in pain or angrily refuse to pray to God in protest. Adults behave no differently than do children. Some adults will find solace in their congregation; others will not be comforted by their congregation as they encounter real or imagined glances and whispers. For this latter group, just at the time when they most need the comfort of communal worship, the desire to attend Sunday services may be nonexistent.

Especially difficult are the situations in which a child or adult prayed to God to prevent the death or divorce, and the worst-feared event happened in spite of the prayer. Such a situation can cause individuals to despair of the existence of God altogether, or a loving God who cares for them personally. This is particularly true of a young child who prayed that everything would be all right, and is, instead, faced with a disaster beyond her imagination.

Individual Responses

When families are disintegrating, friends or neighbors may want to keep their distance. They may not know what to say or to do, or they may not want to intrude. These situations require sensitive approaches. However, if one takes the general rule of asking the family in question what they need, such concerns fade. If a family desires privacy and a time alone to regroup, then that wish should be respected. If the same family wants assistance in errands or child care, then that is what can be offered. The family is the conductor of the orchestra; relatives, friends, and neighbors are only asked to play specific instruments at specific times.

More sympathy is given to a parent and children who lose the other parent through death than through divorce. Yet both families are in shock and grief, and for both, major readjustments must be made. Both need friends. Both groups of children need life to proceed as normally as possible in the midst of chaos. Thus friends and neighbors must explain to their own children in non-judgmental language what has happened to the other family. They can urge their own children to behave normally and not to treat the affected children differently. Unaffected children are called to listen when the affected children want to talk about what has occurred. This is true for parental death, sibling death, or parental divorce. The children who are not directly affected should be cautioned not to pry but to be as open as possible to whatever surfaces. After all, the affected children are still their friends and can remain so.

Parents must watch their own speech, which reflects their inner attitudes, around their children. They should refrain from assigning guilt to one of the divorcing parents or discussing rumors. Furthermore, in the case of a child who died accidentally, the parents should not make remarks about the dead child's parents' ability to care for her, or their irresponsibility in letting an accident occur. If these parents hear their own children making negative remarks or indulging in rumors, they can express their own displeasure and disappointment in such talk.

Adults can befriend the solo parent in ways the solo parent would find helpful. This might mean an occasional dinner or lunch out away from the children. It might also mean going shopping or attending sports or social events with the solo parent. After a death or divorce, the remaining parent may not want to go out at all and certainly may not want to go out alone. Having friends who will accompany him may be a great relief and can assist in healing. Frequently, a simple presence is all that is needed, as the helping individual is ready to listen to words of anger, fear, or grief. However, giving unsolicited advice or taking sides in disagreements is not usually helpful. Keeping the hurting person in prayer is another method of presence for the one who is suffering. Adults can also assist the solo parent by offering to take care of his children while the parent takes some needed private time for himself.

When the death experienced was that of a child, infant, or fetus, the parents may feel too raw to be around other children. If that is the case, they deserve time to grieve and heal. After all, each happy family whom they see reminds them of their own unhappiness and loss. With time, this will heal, but such healing needs to be gradual and natural, not forced or hurried. There is no "official" timetable by which families who have experienced loss have to move; each family is unique. If a child dies, the parents may each heal at different rates, and these rates may be radically different from the rates of healing by the remaining children. Certainly, any grieving parent or child can be assisted by community groups such as Compassionate Friends (a support group for parents whose children have died), bereavement groups for children, and Parents without Partners. Individuals who want to help those in crisis should be familiar with the resources available in their community. Frequently, friends have more psychological energy to research these resources than do the persons who need them the most. In addition, individuals who want to help might also consider volunteering at one of these community services, such as a suicide prevention hotline.

Congregational Responses

Congregations have a role to play in the healing of one of its families. Members of the congregation can visit if the family so wishes. Grieving families note that many people are around during a family member's illness and immediately after the death, but fewer remain for the long haul. Indeed, it is during the weeks after the death that many families need the most support, as the hard reality of their situation finally hits them. In the case of a divorce, many families complain that people shun them as if *they* have done something wrong. Such alienation cannot be condoned in a Christian assembly.

If a child from the congregation has died, the children in the congregation should be informed about the death as sensitively as possible, ideally first by their own parents and then in a group at church or Sunday school. Adults frequently think that children won't notice an absent child or that talking about a death will upset children more than silence, but such adults are wrong. Children are more frightened when nothing is said, because, lacking any facts, they imagine all kinds of terrible events, some of which could happen to them as well. Silence does not make loss easier for children.

By words and actions, the pastor can urge all congregants to place themselves in the position of the family who has experienced a loss. What would they want? Then congregants can be urged to act with hospitality toward that family, always seeking to serve and meet that family's needs rather than fulfill their own needs. The practice of simple presence to those in need can be emphasized. The pastor can also urge all congregants to keep in prayer families who are experiencing loss and can offer public prayers for them (as a group) at weekly liturgies, if the families have given permission for their names to be publicized. Above all, a warning against judging the situations of others must be given. Even in the case of adultery and subsequent divorce, the pastor can remind congregants of Jesus' own actions toward the women caught in adultery; he cautioned others against judging her and refused to judge her himself. In like manner, when Scripture readings permit, the pastor can preach on divorce, highlighting Jesus' own words that Moses permitted divorce because he understood the human heart. Divorce is never ideal, but, in some cases, it really may be the lesser of two evils.

If sufficient numbers of families have experienced loss in the congregation, the pastoral team might consider starting a support group for them, led by a knowledgeable, caring person. The team should be aware of agencies in the community that can provide assistance, so that families can be referred to them if the congregation cannot address those needs itself.

REFERENCES

Anderson, J. "Helping Parents Cope with Sudden Death." *Contemporary Pediatrics* (December 1996), 13:42–57.

Barakat, L., Sills, R., and LaBagnara, S. "Management of Fatal Illness and Death in Children or Their Parents." *Pediatrics in Review* (1995), 16:419–23.

Dell, M. "Divorce—Are You Ready to Help?" *Contemporary Pediatrics* (May 1995), 12:57–68.

Emery, R., and Coiro, M. "Divorce: Consequences for Children." *Pediatrics in Review* (1995), 16:306–10.

Green, M. "Helping Children and Parents Deal with Grief." *Contemporary Pediatrics* (October 1986), 3:84–98.

Kübler-Ross, E. *On Death and Dying.* New York: Macmillan, 1969.

Wallerstein, J., and Johnston, J. "Children of Divorce: Recent Findings Regarding Long-Term Effects and Recent Studies of Joint and Sole Custody." *Pediatrics in Review* (1990), 11:197–203.

STATISTICS

National Center for Health Statistics

www.cdc.gov/nchs/releases/02news/div_mar_cohab.htm
www.cdc.gov/nchs/fastats/death.htm
www.cdc.gov/nchs/fastats/suicide.htm
www.cdc.gov/nchs/fastats/divorce.htm
www.cdc.gov/nchs/releases/02news/div_mar_cohab.htm
www.cdc.gov/nchs/releases/01news/firstmarr.htm

FOR MORE INFORMATION

Check local telephone listings under "Compassionate Friends," "Parents without Partners," "divorce counseling," "support groups," "hospice services," "funeral directors," "bereavement services," and church-sponsored singles groups. Hospice organizations and funeral directors frequently have useful printed information on grief, coping, and so forth.

LOCAL RESOURCES

_____

_____

_____

_____

_____

Chapter 4

Single Parents/Stepfamilies

I don't understand why I have to do so many chores around the apartment," complained 10-year-old Phil. "My friends don't have to do half as much as I do." Said his father, "Phil, I need you to help out because I have to be at work so long. Can't you just do these things for me?" Phil exploded, "I hate you and I hate mom and I hate my life."

Benjamin and his sister Lee were examining the house that they would share with their mother and her new husband and his three children. "I don't want to live here," said 10-year-old Lee. "I'll never call that man my father and I don't like his stupid kids." Fifteen-year-old Benjamin shook his head, "We better try to get along with them. Mom won't like it if we call them names." Lee started to cry, "Why did God let Daddy leave us?"

Physical Challenges

There are a number of unique challenges associated with single parenting. Even though there seems to be more space because of fewer adults in the home, the living area itself is likely to be smaller in size, especially if the single-parent home is led by a mother whose income is less than that of a father. A single parent has no other adult with whom to share the chores, responsibilities, worries, and parenting tasks. An employed single parent must work all day, come home to household chores, and take care of the children as well. This leaves little time for the parent to care for herself or to get some time away for recreation. Time for recreation is critical if the parent and, hence, the children, are to thrive.

Financial worries are also heightened. One salary, particular that of a woman, might not be enough to allow for all the necessities, let alone the luxuries of

Facts to Consider

In addition to children born to single women, both children who have experienced the death of a parent and those who have experienced parental divorce frequently live in single-parent families.

1. In cases of divorce, most children live primarily with their mothers: 51 percent of African American children live with a single mother, as do 27 percent of Hispanic American children and 16 percent of European American children. Only about 3 percent of each ethnic group live solely with their fathers (Emery 306).

2. Childbirth outside marriage is common, with 16 percent of European American children, 32 percent of Hispanic American children, and 61 percent of African American children born to unmarried mothers (Emery 306).

3. The probability of remarriage in five years after divorce is 58 percent for white women, 44 percent for Hispanic women, and 32 percent for black women. Moreover, 81 percent of those divorced before age 25 remarry within ten years compared with 68 percent of those who divorce after age 25 (National Center for Health Statistics).

4. Stepfamilies are a very common type of American family. At present, 20 percent of children under age 18 are stepchildren. Roughly 45 percent of children born during the 1980s experienced the divorce of their parents before they were eighteen years old, and 35 percent of children born in the 1980s lived with a stepparent before they turned eighteen (Visher 146).

life. Children may feel deprived compared with their friends whose families have greater financial resources. They may not be able to have the latest in clothing, music, sports equipment, and the like. It is difficult for a single parent both to make daily ends meet *and* to plan for the future, such as saving for the children's higher education, purchasing a house, and so on. In these families, adolescents may need to get a job, not so much for their own discretionary money, but to assist the family. Children and adolescents may feel embarrassed to bring friends home because their living situations are much more modest than those of their friends.

The single parent also needs to decide how to conduct a social/romantic life. There is evidence that children and teens are confused and resentful when a never-ending stream of friends of the opposite sex visit their parent. They are also likely to be upset if these "dates" take the single parent away from them, and especially if some of these individuals spend the night. Many children and adolescents have great difficulty in thinking of their parents as sexual beings, and so the issue of an adult of the opposite sex sleeping in the parent's bedroom is an emotionally charged one. Even after a divorce, many children desperately want the original parents to reunite. Thus they resent a parent's "special friends."

There are even more physical challenges when two families come together as a result of a second marriage. Two families are usually compelled to live in the space previously occupied by one of them, or at least one family will have *had* to move and become used to a new house, neighborhood, school, and so on. Issues of "what's mine and what's yours" range from bedroom space to combs and clothing. Children previously unrelated to each other may be forced to share bedrooms and bathrooms. Children who previously did not have a brother or sister may now have several. Tempers will flare, especially if the two parents' disciplinary styles vary greatly or if favoritism of any type is detected. The increase in noise level in a previously quiet home of two persons—parent and child—may be very trying if the number of persons has increased greatly and their temperaments are more extroverted. New friends will have to be made, and one family may not like the friends of the other family. In highly dysfunctional families, sexual experimentation between the new siblings may occur.

Emotional Challenges

There is a great deal of responsibility placed on the shoulders of a single parent; in effect, she is trying to be both mother and father to the children. This may not be possible even in the best of circumstances. Hence, single parents may worry about the effect of the lack of a parent of the opposite sex on their children's development. Other worries that a single parent may have include concerns about the adequacy of his parenting, financial issues, job security, health expenses, and the children's futures. Furthermore, there is no one with whom to share these concerns, or even the joys, of parenting.

A single parent is likely to be tired because she is doing the work of two parents. Hence, patience may be limited; frustrations may easily surface. There may be guilt that the child cannot have everything that she wants because of family finances. The single parent is likely to feel alone and underappreciated because the children do not always understand how hard the parent is working to keep life as normal as possible. Arguments between parent and child are common. In addition, if the parent is single because of separation or divorce, the child may make the parent feel guilty or inadequate by saying things like, "I wish Dad were here; he'd know how to fix this." "Why couldn't you and Mom get along—if she were still here, I'd be happier." "Dad's drinking problem wasn't all that bad that you should have left him; I want my father." When a parent is single because of the death of a spouse, children have a little easier time understanding why the deceased parent cannot come back, but they may still resent the fact that they are different from their friends. As the children become older, they may get a better handle on the sacrifices that the single parent is making, but this is not usually the case when children are younger. In the case of a divorce, the child may idolize the absent parent and demonize the remaining one.

Demonizing a new parent is, unfortunately, all too common when two families come together as a result of remarriage. "She doesn't cook like mom did." "He's dumber than my real dad is." "She's too mean." "He's too strict." It almost seems that the new parent cannot do anything correctly, no matter how hard she tries. In addition, the children themselves may be confused about how to address the new parent and whether loving the new parent implies disloyalty to the biological parent. Furthermore, the newly created siblings may dislike each other and vie for parental attention and favor in an attempt to determine who is the favorite child. The insecurity that children face may be exaggerated but must be taken seriously. The children whose house it is may resent the newcomers, who, in turn, may resent having to live in a new house.

Spiritual Challenges

Many single parents have wondered how the set of circumstances in which they find themselves could have happened. "Why did God let me make the mistake of getting pregnant?" "Why did God let me marry such a loser?" "Why doesn't God make my kids appreciate me?" They may also doubt that God will be with them in each and every crisis. Children, too, wonder why they couldn't have two "normal" (or even "wonderful"!) parents like other kids, and if God is punishing them for something they've done. If they have prayed for their situation to change for the better and it does not, they may be disappointed or angry with God.

Spiritual crises are even more complicated in blended families. If the two parents do not share the same religion, there may be confusion among the children as to which religion is "right." Also, if a child idolizes the absent biologic parent, he may want to adopt that parent's religion (even if the parent does not practice it) as a means of identification with him. If the two sets of siblings do not get along, children may wonder why God allowed their parents to marry; they may even pray for them to get divorced and for the original parents to remarry. When that does not happen, their faith in God may be shaken.

Individual Responses

Many of the suggestions for assisting single parents have been explored in the chapter on death and divorce, and need not be repeated here. Individuals who are single parents must monitor their own behavior so that they do not send double messages to their children about sexual relations outside of marriage. Although adults may argue that, as adults, they have the right to conduct their lives as they please, they also have the responsibility to lead their children rightly. Hypocritical behavior, when one's words do not match one's actions, only confuses and eventually alienates children and adolescents. Thus "sleep over" adult friends should not be permitted.

The newly single parent may require much support from friends, as described in the previous chapter, but with time, adjustments to the new lifestyle occur. However, that does not mean that the single parent is never lonely or does not want someone with whom she can socialize. Individuals must be sensitive to the cues sent by the single parent and act accordingly. Certainly, families can get together occasionally for pizza parties or pool parties and the like. One family can offer to keep the single parent's child for the weekend so that the single parent can get away for a much needed rest. Single parents are chronically tired as they juggle work, home chores, and the emotional work of being both parents to the children. Time away is always welcomed if the single parent knows that her children will be safe in her absence. Above all, the single parent needs prayers and adults willing to listen sympathetically. Unsolicited advice and taking sides in disagreements are not usually helpful in the long run.

Individual responses to blended families include hospitality and the refusal to judge their situations. Even if one is convinced that divorce is wrong, one needs to act as Christ would act. All human beings are sinful and have tragic flaws; all human beings are graced. Human beings are not called to take God's unique position of being able to judge someone in love and in justice. Christians are not called to judge but to forgive repeatedly. This behavior is especially important to demonstrate before children and adolescents, who pick up a number of their attitudes from the significant adults in their lives.

Congregational Responses

The congregation might consider developing a support group for single parents if there are sufficient numbers who want to participate. Alternatively, they can give such parents a list of resources in the community at large for single parents.

The problem of blended families is not so obvious. After all, there are two parents present to share the work. However, unless one has experienced a blended family oneself, one does not truly understand the enormous challenges present. At least one of the families has had to move, so that its members must adjust to a new neighborhood, school, and church. They may resent having had to move. After all, it is the adults who want to be together, not necessarily the children. The members of the family whose house is receiving the new members may feel "invaded."

This is where a congregation's prayers and development of a support group are really important. Everyone needs prayers. With the high rate of divorce and remarriage in our society today, as well as the number of remarriages after the death of a spouse, most congregations probably have enough blended families to develop a support group for them. Both children and adults need to realize that they are not the only ones facing these problems; there are plenty of other families in the same predicament. How do others handle disagreements over rooms, discipline, and time with parents? Children *especially* need to know that other kids are facing the same challenges that they are.

Many children and adults are confused by their church's teaching on divorce and remarriage. Is divorce morally wrong? This is where the pastor can play a key role in explaining the church's position (and the reasons for it) in as sensitive a manner as possible, especially for the sake of children who may worry that God doesn't love them or their parents anymore because they are "living in sin." In preaching, the pastor is called to be prophetic, taking a stance against lax sexual behavior and pointing out that, in a perfect world, divorce would be unnecessary. But this is not a perfect world, and human beings are, unfortunately, not perfect either. Without condoning lax sexual mores, the pastor can remind the community of faith that God's love and forgiveness are always available and that these attributes should be mirrored in the responses of committed Christians.

REFERENCES

Emery, R., and Coiro, M. "Divorce: Consequences for Children." *Pediatrics in Review* (1995), 16:306–10.

Visher, E., and Visher, J. "Why Stepfamilies Need Your Help." *Contemporary Pediatrics* (March 1992), 9:146–64.

STATISTICS

National Center for Health Statistics

www.cdc.gov/nchs/releases/02news/div_mar_cohab.htm
www.cdc.gov/nchs/releases/01news/firstmarr.htm

FOR MORE INFORMATION

Check local telephone listings under "Parents without Partners," "divorce counseling," "family counseling," and "support groups."

LOCAL RESOURCES

_____

_____

_____

_____

_____

Chapter 5

Sudden, Unexpected Loss

Virginia is beside herself. While she was not at home, a fire broke out in her house of forty-seven years. Everything was lost. As she stares at her burned-out house, she cries, "I feel like I died. All my pictures are gone; all my memories have gone up in flames."

It happened so fast. The car came around the corner, and the driver didn't see Philip's dog. The dog was killed instantly. Since becoming a widower six years ago, Philip's dog was the only company he had. Now he has nothing. He is numb and angry when his friends tell him, "It was *only* a dog."

Several days before her fortieth birthday, Candace arrived for work in a celebratory mood. She was looking forward to the weekend away that she was giving herself as a treat for her birthday. But her joy was shattered several hours later. Candace was one of twenty-five employees laid off in a down-sizing move by her company. "How could this happen to me?" she wondered, "I've been a faithful employee for twenty-three years—since I graduated from high school. I don't know how to do anything but work here. I can't go away for my weekend now! I don't even know how I'm going to pay the bills in another month or so. Who's going to hire me?"

Physical Challenges

The physical challenges associated with loss vary. A house fire or lightning strike that destroys one's dream house or one's childhood home means that one must find a new dwelling in which to live. In addition, one might have to replace needed possessions such as clothing and personal items as well as household items. Even though certain items can be replaced through insurance reimbursement, the original items (and their meaning) can never be replaced. Thus the loss of personal mementos such as photos, letters, handmade items, family heirlooms, gifts, and so forth, might be devastating because there *is* no possibility of replacement.

Loss of a pet means the loss of the physical presence of the pet and the routines that were associated with its care, such as walking it, grooming it, and so forth. Items associated with the pet—such as its cage, food bowl, food, toys, and leash—are a constant reminder that the pet is gone. The sights and sounds associated with the pet are forever gone. For many persons who are homebound, pets are the only consistent company that they might have had; their pets have been their friends. The loss of a pet can be as devastating to them as the loss of a human friend.

Loss of a job is particularly traumatic. In this country we are defined by what we do. When we meet someone for the first time, we frequently ask, "And what do you do?" or "Where do you work?" In our society, people without jobs are lacking something that most adults have. To lose a job suddenly is to lose one's position in society. It is also to lose one's daily routine and a small space that one calls one's own in a workplace.

> ### General Comments
>
> Sudden loss *is* jarring. Most of us are creatures of habit; we like our routines and that which is familiar to us. When we lose the familiar, especially if we have had no time to prepare ourselves for the trauma, the loss can be devastating.
>
> Suddenly losing a familiar pet, object, or place might be as wrenching for some people as losing a person is for others. That which we hold dear in some way defines us and gives us our meaning. To lose that which is dear—even if it is not a person—is to lose something of ourselves.
>
> Every year in this country, people suddenly lose their houses through fires or acts of nature; their pets through motor-vehicle accidents, other accidents, or illnesses; their jobs through downsizing, bankruptcy, or their own actions; and their savings through stock-market plunges. Although one might debate whether people should be so attached to material objects, judgment is not what is most needed at the time of the loss. All these things *are* important to those who have lost them.

Emotional Challenges

Inherent in any loss is the idea that something precious, something that gives a person meaning, is gone. This is true regardless of whether the loss is a pet, a house, a job, or anything else of importance.

When one loses something of great value, one must mourn. Mourning takes place at its own rate and is dependent on the significance of the object that was lost. The significance of that which is lost is a very individual thing, and one cannot tell others that they should or should not be so distraught about their loss. Usually this type of advice is given to cheer someone up, but the opposite might happen if the person experiencing the loss gets the sense that the well-wisher doesn't understand at all or is trivializing either that which was lost or the connection between what was lost and the grieving person. Sometimes people who have lost something quite significant in their lives are made to feel foolish and childish because of the lack of understanding of those around them.

It is natural to feel as if one has lost a significant piece of oneself, especially if the loss was a home, pet, or job. Hence, one might fear that one's security is lost, especially if one identified closely with the object lost. It is human to want to surround ourselves with that which gives us meaning, pleasure, and security. In the case of the loss of a job, uninsured home, or finances, one might be facing a grave financial crisis. With a loss, there might also be a complete sense of disorientation. For example, one must learn to drive to a new house or get used to an entirely new environment. Or one might have to begin a new job with all of its idiosyncrasies and duties. One's former neighbors and former coworkers must be left behind. Everything must be learned anew; new contacts must be made.

There is a great deal of emotional stress associated with the newness of another house or job. This might lead to fatigue. Because fatigue might also be part of mourning, especially if it is accompanied by depression, persons experiencing the loss might have an even greater degree of fatigue. Just when they need all the energy they can muster to learn the demands of a new job or to become accustomed to a new house, they have no energy or are "always tired." Perhaps they are not sleeping or eating as well as they need to be; perhaps they are not getting the proper amount of exercise.

The worse they feel, the more discouraged they can become. This is particularly worrisome because when someone is starting anew, discouragement is an impediment to success. And for the losses that are being described here, starting anew is what is needed. When a house is destroyed, one must start anew in a different house; when one loses a job, one must start anew in a different job; when one loses a pet, one must start anew without the pet or with a new one. Starting anew is difficult at any time but is particularly difficult for the aged, those lacking resources, and those who have failed multiple times in the past. Maybe this time the person won't be able to bounce back.

No matter how wonderful, a new house, job, or pet cannot replace what was treasured and lost—at least, not in the beginning. Hence, depending on the person who has experienced the loss, it might be completely inappropriate to say, "You can get a new job"; or "Go to the animal shelter and get a new dog"; or "I thought you said you hated your old house—now you have a new one." Although a new house, job, or pet might become far more rewarding than the old one, that is not the way it usually seems in the beginning.

Spiritual Challenges

Sudden loss engenders many questions about whether one is being tested by God. A minister once told his congregation, "Any affection for material things is wrong. Your concern should be for God alone. When we lose something or someone, God is testing us to see if God is first or if something else is first."

If God knows everything, God certainly doesn't need to test us to see if we will pass the test or not. Of course, such testing might be so that *we* can gain a greater insight as to where our priorities lie. Nevertheless, such a concept of testing harkens back to the Book of Job when Satan argued that if God took away the goods that Job had, Job would fail the test and turn away from God. This is not a very sympathetic portrait of God, a God whom Jesus noted had counted the hairs on our heads and knew our needs before we did.

Human beings seek to find meaning in the events of their lives. When they experience a traumatic event such as a loss of something significant, the loss must have a greater purpose. That is the reason that many people speculate that their loss is because God is testing them, purifying them, or punishing them for some transgression—real or imagined. For many people, even a negative meaning is better than no meaning at all. For example, a tornado destroys a house. Rather than believe that it was "just" an act of nature, some people will speculate that God was punishing them for having a big house while poor people have nowhere to live. Or consider someone who loses a job in a downsizing. Rather than believe that the job loss was "just" another result of a weakened economy, some might speculate that because God felt it was the wrong job for a person, God took the job away so that the person would *have* to get a better position. Or consider the elderly couple who loses much of their retirement savings in a stock-market scandal. Rather than attribute their loss to the dishonesty of traders or corporate executives, some people might speculate that God was testing this couple to see if their trust was in God alone. These approaches might not be the most beneficial and frankly might be harmful to a suffering person's understanding of God.

The question of "Why me?" rises to the forefront of *any* discussion of loss, especially if the person experiencing the loss has tried to live an upright life.

Why do bad things happen to good people? Why doesn't God step in to change things—or, at least, send a warning to one about to lose something valuable? Unfortunately, on this side of heaven, there are no pat answers.

Individual Responses

When learning about someone experiencing a loss, individuals should refrain from making judgments about whether the person's response is appropriate, for that is not for others to say. Instead, a simple "I'm sorry to hear about your loss; is there something that I can do for you?" is the best sentiment one could express. One always asks what is needed rather than making a speculation based on one's own needs. Depending on the loss and what the person says he or she needs, an individual might provide temporary shelter when a house has been destroyed, lend money when there has been a financial crisis, pass the person's name on to potential employers when a job has been lost, or offer to help the person get a new pet when a pet has died. In addition, one can always pray for the person and offer whatever moral support is needed. Many times, this means the simple gift of empathetic listening, a gift so needed and appreciated but so infrequently offered.

Congregational Responses

Every congregation has a prayer list; usually, this list names the ill or dying. But there is no reason why the list could not be expanded to name anyone in need of prayer or anyone experiencing a loss. Of course, the permission of those listed (or named aloud at a service) will need to be solicited before the public listing or announcing of any person's name. The pastor and other pastoral leaders could remind congregants to keep these individuals in prayer during the week.

For one of its own experiencing a loss, with that person's permission a congregation can take up a special collection, organize a bake or craft sale, car wash, or the like, or encourage individual donations by congregants. The early Christian church shared resources among all members, and the modern church is also called to share resources with those in its midst most in need. Other donations might not be monetary, such as donations of clothing or housewares (for someone who has lost items in a fire), food (for someone who has lost his or her job), or a new pet (for someone who has recently lost a pet *and* wants a new one).

Pastoral leaders should know the contact information for organizations in their community that assist people in need, such as the Red Cross, Meals on Wheels, and so forth. In order to make the most appropriate referrals, they should also be aware of what the criteria are in order to receive assistance. Also, members of the congregation could be available to accompany anyone making an appointment with any of these agencies to help the individuals in whatever way seems best. As was mentioned previously, many of the people suffering loss are discouraged and fatigued; having someone to be with them as they fill out forms and answer questions is a great gift.

Knowing individuals within the congregation with certain needed skills is essential and can be quite helpful in meeting the needs of persons experiencing loss. If there is a realtor in the congregation, she might be able to locate an affordable house for someone who has lost a house. If there is a career counselor, he might be able to give advice to the person who has lost his job. If there is a financial planner or an accountant, she might be able to assist someone who has lost savings in bad investing. If there is someone who has access to pets, he might be able to secure a new pet for someone who has lost a pet. Knowing the skills of congregants might mean that a person in need of assistance could speak to someone whom he knows rather than to strangers. However, keep in mind that some persons would rather speak to strangers than to those who know them in order to preserve their privacy and their dignity.

If a number of people in a congregation have lost their jobs, a support group might be started. In addition, information on job fairs in the community could be shared so that these individuals are kept informed about ways to move beyond their current status.

An annual special service in honor of God's creation could be organized. At such a service, pets (and their owners) could receive a blessing, and pets that have died (and their owners) could be remembered in prayer. In addition, a special, annual service for anyone experiencing any kind of loss in the past year could be provided. In both cases, the services would be open to all who would want to come, a wonderful reminder that in the body of Christ, we are all one—in both prosperity and misfortune, in both laughter and pain, in both good times and bad.

FOR MORE INFORMATION

Check local telephone listings under "Red Cross," "Salvation Army," "career counseling," "employment," "job services/training," "food/clothing/fuel assistance," "pet adoption," "animal shelters," "humane society," and "support groups."

LOCAL RESOURCES

_____

_____

_____

_____

_____

Chapter 6

Moving

Seth was the lead altar server at his church when his father received word that his company was transferring him to another city. Seth ran away from home to avoid moving, but was too frightened to go far and returned home on his own. Now that the family has moved, Seth refuses to go to church. "I don't want to start all over," he complained. "I knew where everything was at my old church. I liked Reverend Bob (his previous pastor). Church will never be the same. If God really cares about us, He would have let me stay where I was so happy."

Physical Challenges

Moving requires a great deal of physical effort because of the great amount of possessions that the average U.S. family has. Packing, lifting, and unpacking boxes is laborious and tedious. Once the move is made, not being sure exactly where one's belongings are is disconcerting. Adjusting to a new house or apartment, no matter how nice it is, takes time and patience.

In addition, the family that moves will need to find new places to shop, work, recreate, and worship. Many attempts are trial-and-error before the most suitable sites are found. One of the most difficult adjustments is to find new schools and new health-care providers, especially if the previous ones were much beloved.

Physical adjustment might be even more difficult when the move takes a family from one climate to another (e.g., from the southwest to the east coast) or when a move is to or from a foreign country. When a move is to a foreign country, multiple adjustments will need to be made in terms of becoming acclimated to different customs, language, food, and dress.

Emotional Challenges

It is difficult to leave one's friends behind. If this is difficult for an adult who understands the reasons for a move, such as a change of employment or change of marital status, how much harder it is for a child who cannot make sense of the repeated moves that his father's employer places upon the family, or the reasons why a mother and her children have to move out of the family house after a divorce. Children like routine—in school, in playmates, in after-school activities, and so forth. Moves upset children's sense of routine and may give them the sense that nothing can be depended upon, that nothing is permanent.

Children are likely to miss their friends deeply. They may not be able to communicate with them through letter writing because they are too young to write or by telephone if family finances are tight. Thus a child may feel that her world has been destroyed.

Children have to make adjustments to a new school, new teachers, and new classmates. It is very difficult for most children to be the "new kid" in class. For shy children, it is especially painful. Although new children in class want to make friends, they do not like to be singled out for special treatment: "Johnny is new to our class. Who will eat lunch with him today?" Such adult attempts at socializing children may backfire as the class resents having to help the new child and the new child resents needing help. Children pine for their old school, where they knew all the staff, the layout of the building, and the daily routine. Of most importance, children especially miss particularly beloved teachers and classmates.

When the move was not wanted by the child or when it is the tragic side effect of a marital breakup or the death of a parent, there will be more grieving than if the child welcomed the move. Grief can take many forms, such as crying and depression, acting out behaviorally, school failure, or loss of interest in friends or social activities. Because some children are shy and find it very difficult to make new friends, moving may be an excruciatingly painful experience.

Facts to Consider

1. Each year, 20 percent of families move, and two-thirds of U.S. children have moved at least once in their lifetimes (Fowler 934).

2. Only one-third of the U.S. civilian population has never moved, whereas one-third has moved one or two times, and one-third has moved three or more times.

3. At any given point in time, 21 percent of the population have been at their current address less than 12 months, 17 percent have lived at their current address 12–35 months, and 55 percent have lived at their current address 36 months or more (Fowler 935).

Spiritual Challenges

The spiritual challenges of a move are both personal and corporate. On the personal level, the adults and especially children struggle to understand why such an uprooting was necessary. "Is any job worth having to move?" asked one frustrated 8-year-old child. Younger children may wonder if God knows where they have moved, whereas older children may wonder how the move will affect their lives and why God allowed it. They may be angry at God if they prayed not to have to move, or they may wonder if God even exists.

On a corporate level, moving requires a family to find a new church at which to worship. This is, of course, not just a building, but a congregation, congenial to the beliefs of the family and children. Sometimes, families quickly happen upon the ideal church for them; at other times, months and even years go by before the right congregation is located, if ever. For example, families need to assess new congregations by asking themselves which attributes are critical for them. How welcoming is the new congregation? Are minorities welcomed? Does the congregation have a diverse membership, or is it more homogeneous than family members would like? Is the congregation more conservative or liberal? How do the congregants and the pastor treat children? Divorced parents?

Children who were deeply involved in their church's activities may also miss them, and, like Seth, refuse to attend a new church because it will never be the same. Indeed, Seth's running away, albeit temporarily, and his anger are not unusual reactions.

Individual Responses

From time immemorial, neighbors have welcomed newcomers to their neighborhoods with friendship, food, and gifts. And that will continue. The individual's response to the newcomer should be one of hospitality as revealed in Scripture—both the Hebrew Scriptures and the New Testament. To be able to greet and serve a stranger was thought to be a great honor. As we learn in the New Testament, people's interest in welcoming Jesus into their homes for meals led to his dubious reputation as a "glutton and a drunkard" because he readily accepted these invitations.

Congregational Responses

Any congregation that expects to grow must seek and welcome newcomers. Hospitality must be the hallmark of any Christian community, and the pastoral team can model this behavior to their congregants. In addition, the pastor can preach on the meaning of hospitality (and the practical ways it is demonstrated), especially on those Sundays when the Scripture readings describe hospitality.

How does the congregation welcome its new members? Are they publicly recognized at worship services? Are they afforded a reception following that service so that others can meet them? How often do such welcoming events occur in a given congregation?

How does the congregation evangelize newcomers in its tract? Ideally, it is done through personal contact by congregants and not necessarily the pastor. After all, newcomers want to know from fellow congregants what the church and its people are really like, and many people think that is best discovered from one's prospective fellow congregants.

How easy is it for new parishioners to learn about a church's various committees? How easy is it for new congregants to explore various ministries, such as reading at liturgy? How does the church express its desire for the participation of new members? Does the church seek them, or does the church expect new members to make the first move?

Does the congregation encourage all of its members to evangelize? Does it have printed materials about itself to give to newcomers? Does it have someone in the church office on most days to answer questions about the times of worship or directions to the church? In lieu of a person at the telephone seven days a week, is there a friendly taped message providing the same information? It is in these small but significant ways that a congregation can identify itself as possessing the hospitality of Christ.

And let's not forget the children. How are new children incorporated into the life of the church? How easy is it for them to enter a religious education class or Sunday school? What welcoming ceremonies are in place for them there? Teaching children at an early age about hospitality is an important step in sensitizing them to the Christian witness of hospitality. As children see adults extending hospitality to newcomers, they learn that the norm is to welcome those who are new or different rather than to remain separate from them. That is as it should be, because all are members of one family—the family of God.

REFERENCES

Fowler, M., Simpson, G., and Schoendorf, K. "Families on the Move and Children's Health Care." *Pediatrics* (1993), 91:934–40.

FOR MORE INFORMATION

Check the local telephone listings under "movers," "moving," and "relocation services."

LOCAL RESOURCES

_____

_____

_____

_____

_____

Chapter 7

Chronic Conditions, Catastrophic Illnesses, and Health Insurance

Seven-year-old Maxie is missing another day of school. Diagnosed with asthma at age 2, he has been admitted seventeen times to the local children's hospital for flare-ups of his condition. Every day, he must take multiple medications, both by mouth and through a breathing machine. Maxie hates missing school, but his mother knows that the unusually hot, humid weather on this October day will cause her son to wheeze as soon as he goes out. She prefers to keep him home . . . and inside.

Walter used to have a good job as a roofer. But an unstable ladder gave way while Walter was climbing it, and he fell to the ground, breaking his neck. Now, at age 35, he is paralyzed from the midchest down. He feels as if he is only a burden to his family. He sometimes wishes that he had died in the accident.

After being laid off in her company's downsizing initiative, Cherise now works as a temporary secretary. Although she makes a reasonable salary, the agency for which she works does not offer her health benefits. Cherise cannot afford the several hundred dollars a month it would cost for her to buy health insurance for herself and her twin daughters. So she prays that they all stay healthy and dreams of the time when she will have a job that will provide her with health benefits.

ᔕᔕᔕᔕᔕᔕ

Physical Challenges

Obviously, the type of chronic condition or injury that a person has will determine the kinds and severity of the physical challenges faced by a family. A

49

General Comments

A chronic illness is defined as any condition lasting at least twenty-eight days. The types of conditions and their severity vary by age. Overall, the most common, serious chronic illnesses are heart disease, cancer, lung disease (including asthma), degenerative diseases, and arthritis. Most chronic illnesses are managed on an outpatient basis, with only occasional (if any) admissions to a hospital.

A catastrophic condition is one with the capacity to devastate the patient, physically and emotionally, and to wipe out family savings because of the expensive nature of the medical treatment. Some examples are these: aftermath of a major motor-vehicle accident; birth of a severely ill or deformed child; AIDS; cancer, especially if treated with chemotherapy or bone marrow transplant; aftermath of a stroke; aftermath of a severe heart attack; and aftermath of a serious infection that has left a person neurologically compromised. If a person survives a catastrophic event, he or she is frequently left with chronic health conditions or limitations.

Chronic illnesses and conditions require a change in the way a person and his or her family lives, works, plays, and even worships. The financial burdens associated with chronic illnesses include the cost of medications, special medical equipment, special at-home nursing care, and visits to the doctor, clinic, or hospital (e.g., transportation, parking, meals, up-front/out-of-pocket fees). They can also include the loss of income.

Facts to Consider

1. Almost one-third of U.S. children younger than age 18 have a chronic health condition that is expected to last more than three months. Five percent of U.S. children have such chronic conditions that limit their age-appropriate performance in school or at play (Liptak 64).

2. Over a third of the children who were of very low birthweight have school difficulties compared with 14 percent of other children.

3. In one study, 30 percent of children with a chronic condition repeated a grade, and 34 percent received special services in school. In another study, 14 percent of children with chronic illnesses had severe reading problems compared with 4.5 percent of healthy children (Liptak 64–5).

4. Over 68 million U.S. citizens have some kind of activity limitations; 19 million have visual impairments (including three million with glaucoma and 700,000 with cataracts); and 34 million have hearing impairments. Nearly three million U.S. citizens are speech impaired (National Center for Health Statistics).

5. Nationally, 40.5 million U.S. citizens under age 65 are without health insurance (uninsured or underinsured), including 12 percent of all U.S. children. Uninsured means *no* insurance coverage at all, whereas underinsured means some insurance coverage, but with substantial out-of-pocket payment for oneself or family members.

There are several reasons why so many people do not have adequate coverage:

- Employers with few employees do not have to offer insurance as a benefit.
- Seasonal jobs and part-time jobs do not have to include health insurance as a benefit.
- Buying insurance on one's own is expensive, especially for a family.

People think that they will stay healthy and avoid the expense of health insurance. The working poor are caught in a bind—parents are working at entry-level jobs that do not offer health-care benefits. Sometimes a worker is insured, but her children are not (Newacheck 28).

family whose child has been born with a congenital defect may face a lifetime of health problems, whereas the adult with an injury due to a fall may experience physical challenges until recovery. Some acute illnesses and injuries evolve into chronic conditions, such as the aftermath of meningitis (an infection around the covering of the brain and spinal cord), that may lead to deafness or mental retardation, or the residual effects of a diving accident after which the victim is paralyzed below the neck. In addition, older individuals suffer strokes, which, even with rehabilitation, might leave the person with deficits in her ability to function independently. Such chronic conditions have implications not only for the involved party but also for those who must care for her. For example, the physical plant of the house may need to be changed to accommodate a wheelchair. A parent may have to give up employment to care for an ill child. Oxygen tanks may have to be installed in a bedroom. Feeding by gravity and tube may have to be initiated into an already full schedule.

It should also be mentioned that chronic mental conditions may also necessitate physical changes. For example, the person who is chronically depressed cannot be left alone because he might hurt himself, or the elderly person with Alzheimer's disease cannot be left alone because she might start a fire in the house. A violent child might need built-in restraints to safeguard himself and other family members.

If health insurance is lacking or deficient, the money to pay for needed equipment, therapies, and continued physician visits might stretch family resources to the limit. Such a situation will necessitate a financial sacrifice on the part of a family to be able to afford needed equipment or therapies. Alternatively, a family member may have to take on another job to pay for these items, leaving less time for other members of the family.

Emotional Challenges

The stress of a chronic condition or catastrophic injury is, of course, a stress on the affected person. When an affected person is old enough and aware enough, he will realize what he lacks in abilities compared to others or what he has lost in abilities compared to his former self; he will also realize what alterations his family has had to make for him. This may lead to depression and despair about the family's circumstances and his own condition. In addition, if health insurance coverage is an issue, the ill person may worry about how bills will be paid or if necessary therapies and equipment will be available when needed. This is especially true if the family's financially responsible member has openly expressed these concerns in the presence of the ill individual.

A chronically ill person in a household may engender resentment. Children may resent that they can't have their friends over or run about or raise their voices in the house because of the ill family member. Teens may be embarrassed to have their friends over especially if the ill person acts in an immature fashion or has peculiar odors. Adults may be too tired to entertain and thus may limit their social circle. Isolation and overwhelming fatigue may mark the emotional response of family members who have experienced an ill member for a long time. They may wonder what life would be like when the ill person dies (or had never been born) and then may experience guilt for such thoughts. These normal emotions occur even when the ill person is truly loved and cherished by the other family members.

Young children may resent the amount of time their parents must dedicate to the ill family member and may act out as a cry for attention. Teens may stay out beyond their curfews or get heavily involved in extracurricular activities in an attempt to stay away from home. The working parent may work extra shifts for the same reasons. Family members may get involved in substance abuse in order to escape from the hard realities of their lives.

The stress of having a family member who may act inappropriately (in the case of mental conditions) or may act dangerously is a source of constant worry for all family members. As one child said, "Every time I go to school, I worry if we'll even have a house after they leave grandpa there all day long. He likes to smoke but sometimes he doesn't remember to put out his matches."

Spiritual Challenges

Many persons facing health crises in their families turn to God for needed support and strength. Yet, in the tradition of the psalmist, they may ask, "Why, Lord?" "Why my child?" "Why my parent?" "Why did he have to drive his car so fast?" "Why couldn't the doctors have done something to help him?" "Why must she smoke?" "Why are my children acting up?"

Faith in a good and loving God may be pushed to the limit as these questions are posed. "If God is loving and powerful, why doesn't God cure AIDS?" "Just when we need the extra money, why did God let my husband get hurt?" "What's the use in praying? If we're in trouble, it must be God's will."

A caregiver's attendance at church may be curtailed because an ill family member cannot be left at home alone and because the caregiver's prayer life is dwindling. With less church attendance, social contacts made through the church become limited. Caught in a self-perpetuating cycle, a caregiver is reluctant to go to the very place where she can receive spiritual and social nourishment. Alienation from God may grow deeper.

Individual Responses

Individuals can send cards to, telephone, and visit church members who are hospitalized or who are at home recovering from illnesses, injuries, and surgeries. Assurances of continuing prayers are important. These gestures may seem minor, but they may mean a great deal to those who need the comfort of a kind voice and smile. Congregants should always call first to determine what gestures the ill person and his family would find the most helpful. Cards, calls, and visits are welcomed not only to an ill family member but to her caregiver as well. A caregiver needs to know that social and personal support is available and may be relieved to know that someone is willing to run some errands, shop for the family, or assume child care for an afternoon or evening.

Congregational Responses

The congregation as a whole can train some of its members as ministers to the ill. Naturally, this training must be done by someone who is well aware of the issues surrounding sudden illness, terminal illness, and catastrophic illness. This may mean that training is best accomplished using diocesan/denominational or community resources rather than the limited resources of an individual congregation. These ministers to the ill can be commissioned before the entire congregation at a Sunday service. Then, periodically (according to the custom of the denomination), they can take Eucharist to the ill members or conduct prayer services in the home. These ministers can also notify the pastor and the pastoral staff when the situation warrants a pastor's visit. Pastors cannot visit all the people that they want to in the best of circumstances, so these ministers to the ill can be a great help to the pastor and a great comfort to ill persons and their families.

Naturally, ill members of the congregation can be remembered in prayers at each worship service, by name if they so desire. In addition, there can be a reminder in the church bulletin for all members to pray for the ill (named) during the week. This is especially true for those whose dying is prolonged. In the case of cancer, AIDS, or the aftermath of a severe stroke, the dying process may take months and sometimes years, a reality that those who are healthy sometimes forget. A public call to prayer for those who are terminally ill reminds those who are healthier to keep their brothers and sisters in their prayers. This is especially important for those with AIDS, who, along with their families, may feel disregarded or condemned by society as a whole as well as by individual friends and relatives.

Healing services at church are also wonderful ways for congregations to enter into the lives of their ill members. After all, we are *all* ill in body, mind, or spirit at some time in our lives and so are in need of each other's prayers. Depending on the denomination, the healing service will have a particular style and rhythm, and certain readings and hymns will be more meaningful than will others. Such services should be designed with congregational needs in mind. A good point to raise in a sermon at this type of service is the difference between healing and cure. A cure is the eradication of the physical problem, such as a tumor's disappearance or a stroke victim's resumption of normal speech. Healing is much more holistic: it includes body, mind, and spirit. One can be healed but not cured, as in the case of a dying person who is at peace in body, mind, and spirit. One can be cured but not healed, as in the case of a drunk driver who survives his nearly fatal accident only to drink and drive again. Although a physical cure might be what is most desired, healing of all involved might be enduring.

Socially, the congregation can conduct a white sale, car wash, or special dinner to raise money for one of its own who is facing hard times and lacking the financial resources to cover expenses. In this way, children, adolescents, and adults can work as a team for one of their own. It is a wonderful way for young people to learn the real meaning of the body of Christ—that one member cares for an ailing member so that the entire body can return to wholeness. Such a graphic lesson can remind young people that we are all members of the body of Christ. It can also remind all members of Jesus' own remarkable ministry as he went out of his way to care for the ill people of his time. His is an example for all.

REFERENCES

Liptak, G., and Weitzman, M. "Children with Chronic Conditions Need Your Help at School." *Contemporary Pediatrics* (September 1995), 12:64–80.
Newacheck, P., Hughes, D., and Stoddard, J. "Children's Access to Primary Care: Differences by Race, Income, and Insurance Status." *Pediatrics* (1996), 97:26–32.

STATISTICS

National Center for Health Statistics

www.cdc.gov/nchs/fastats/dsable.htm
www.cdc.gov/nchs/fastats/hinsure.htm

FOR MORE INFORMATION

Check local telephone listings under "disabilities," "developmental disabilities," "hearing services," "vision impairment services," "speech services," "support groups," "health agencies and organizations"—private and govern-ment, "social services," and "veterans services."

National Toll-Free Numbers

Alzheimer's	1-800-443-2273
Cancer	1-800-422-6237
Diabetes	1-800-342-2383
American Heart Association	1-800-242-8721
American Lung Association	1-800-560-2120

LOCAL RESOURCES

Chapter 8

Aging

*J*eanne hates living in a nursing home, but since her stroke, her children have convinced her that she can no longer live alone. "But why can't I live with one of you?" she asks. "Why can't you take care of me like I took care of you when you were kids?"

James lives with his daughter's family, but the children are so noisy that they interrupt his sleep. He likes his room at her house—if only the children would settle down so he could nap during the day. But he's afraid to say anything, because he is grateful that he has a family who will look after him and not send him to a nursing home.

Physical Challenges

Older persons may have a number of physical complaints that were not present when they were younger. Although many older people are free of such complaints, the majority of older persons experience some of these conditions. Stiffness of the muscles or joints may limit one's mobility. Blood pressure abnormalities and cardiac problems may limit a person's ability to handle routine tasks, limit one's diet, or limit one's ability to have a satisfying sexual life. Decreased lung capacity may effectively limit one's ability to perform only the most minor of household chores. Mild forgetfulness may cause one to miss important engagements or to forget to pay bills on time; prolonged reaction time may limit one's ability to drive far distances or at night. Limitations in eyesight or hearing may make it impossible to read as much as one likes or to hear normal conversation.

For some older persons, the physical challenges are much more marked. Stroke patients may be paralyzed or confined to a wheelchair. They may have lost the ability to communicate or to see. Chronic years of diabetes may render a person visually impaired or have affected the circulation in his legs, so that independent mobility is very difficult. Severe pulmonary disease may keep a person prisoner in his own house, because he becomes winded after even minor exertion or requires oxygen. Persons with Alzheimer's disease may have lost all vestiges of their previous selves.

Special equipment may be needed for day-to-day living, such as oxygen tanks, walkers, portable toilets, special beds or chairs, wheelchairs, or seeing-eye dogs. Known surroundings may have been altered to accommodate these items. Alternatively, the older person may have had to move out of familiar surroundings if such adaptation could not take place. Adjustments may be particularly difficult if the older person must live with a younger relative or in a nursing home against her will. In addition, loved ones and friends may themselves have become ill or died, leaving the older person relatively alone.

> **Facts to Consider**
>
> It is very disconcerting to be aging in a culture such as ours that devalues the contributions that older persons have made to our society, preferring, instead, to worship the young and/or ablebodied. Whether from media or even the corporate world, the message is given, "Young is best."
>
> 1. There were 35 million U.S. citizens aged 65 and older in 2000; that number is expected to double by the year 2030 (U.S. census data).
>
> 2. Currently, there are 4.3 million persons aged 85 and older; by 2030, if current trends continue, there will be 19 million in that age category (Bronfenbrenner 212).
>
> 3. In 2000, there were 20 million women and 14 million men over age 65, a ratio of three to two (U.S. Census Data).
>
> 4. About 7 million U.S. citizens over age 65 depend on others for help with activities of daily living (Bronfenbrenner 221).
>
> 5. In 2000, 1.6 million U.S. citizens over age 65 were living in nursing homes (National Center for Health Statistics), while millions more live with family members or friends.

Emotional Challenges

For those older persons who can remember how life used to be, there is sometimes a deep sadness for what was once but is no more. They mourn the loss of loved ones and friends and their own physical stamina. They mourn the once vibrant abilities that have become lost with age.

There is also the sadness that comes with knowing that one is no longer really considered a useful member of society. The once astute business executive is now confined to his bed; no one wants his opinion any longer. The person who was once the life of every party is now never invited to any parties. No one even visits her. This feeling of uselessness may be especially heightened in those who spend their days in nursing homes. Bereft of familiar surroundings, an older person in a nursing home may feel especially alienated if family or friends do not visit. She may wonder what she has done to deserve her current situation. In her sadness, she may become weepy. Alternatively, she may become obstreperous, difficult to get along with, even under the best of circumstances. Although such anger is understandable, given the circumstances, it does not help those who work with such individuals. In fact, it may push potential new friends and helpers away.

If significant persons in an older person's life have died, he may keenly miss their companionship. He may mourn the loss of the deep feelings he could once share with significant individuals in his life, and that, he fears, will never be appreciated by anyone else again.

If an older person suffers from a psychiatric disorder or an organic brain disorder, she may become paranoid or highly suspicious of the intentions of those who visit or attempt to help.

There might be a great sense of fear and dread—fear of abandonment by one's family, church, friends, and even God; fear of pain; fear of continued diminishment of abilities; fear of living in a nursing home; fear of abuse at the hands of caregivers; and fear of death, especially fear of dying alone. Persons with particular conditions may have specific fears. For example, chronic heart disease or several heart attacks may leave affected individuals with an overwhelming fear that any exertion will kill them; thus they become afraid to engage in active living again.

Some older persons may have such a longing for the past that they completely discount anything in the present, such as current music, fashion styles, religious leaders, political leaders, books, theater, and so forth. Refusing to participate in any social activities, they remove themselves from potential friends who might be able to be with them and whose company they might enjoy.

There may also be regrets over what an older person may have wanted to accomplish in her life that now seems impossible. This sense of regret may be coupled with a sense of resentment, especially if she perceives that she had been prevented from achieving goals by persons or circumstances beyond her control. She might resent those who are still young enough to achieve their goals.

Spiritual Challenges

As many older persons look back, they may be struck by the way that God has been so present throughout their lives. They may be deeply grateful for their gifts, their families, and their friends. They are not eager to die, but they are eager to see what God continues to have in store for them.

Other older persons have a decidedly more negative view. They blame God for their failing health and their failed dreams. Instead of seeing God as the Source of all that is good, they view God as the genesis of their problems. They may be angry at God, refusing to pray even in the midst of their loneliness. Alternatively, they may deny the existence of God. They are alienated not only from other persons but also from God. In the end, they are alienated from themselves.

Some older persons may fear dying because they fear God's punishment for real or imagined wrongs committed in their lives. They may say things like "I bet God has never seen a sinner like me"; or "It's too late for me"; or "I'm too bad to be forgiven for all that I've done." Such statements cause them to resist dying with all their energies. Each decrement in physical ability reminds them that they will not live forever and that the end draws nearer. They live in fear and dread.

For one reason or another, older persons may have ceased attending church services. The reasons range from physical immobility to spiritual despair, as typified by such comments as "What's the use? God doesn't hear my prayers"; or "I don't like the way the church has changed these days"; or "I can pray just as well at home"; or "I don't like those nosy people always asking me how I am—they're just hypocrites." In their lives, the church and congregational worship play no role. They erect impenetrable walls around themselves. If God cannot reach them, how can mere mortals?

Individual Responses

Many persons do not like to associate with older persons because they are reminded of their own aging. Others do not like to associate with older persons because they have been convinced by the media that old people are foolish, senile, or have nothing to teach them. What a tragic mistake! In many cultures, especially those in the Orient, older people are venerated as repositories of wisdom. It is too bad that many Western people are so shortsighted that they think wisdom is unnecessary when people are technologically advanced.

Individuals can examine their own attitudes toward those who are older, and why they believe the way they do. They can examine whether they have unwittingly passed these attitudes on to the children in their lives. Similarly, older people can examine their own attitudes toward younger people, and why they have these attitudes. It is only by honest self-appraisal that differences in attitude can be corrected.

Caring individuals can make an attempt to communicate with older persons by card or telephone, letting them know that they remain in their prayers. They might also consider visiting them or running errands for them, if the older persons so desire. This includes not only older persons in their own homes but those in nursing homes as well. It is vitally important to discern what an older person wants or needs before making assumptions. After all, these individuals are adults, not children, who have their own preferences. For some older persons, the prospect of a visitor or someone running an errand for them will come as a great relief, a gift. For others, it will seem intrusive or remind them that they are not as capable of handling their own affairs as they once were. Walking lightly in such circumstances is the Christ-like behavior.

Congregational Responses

Because many older persons are not able to drive, a congregation can set up a transportation ministry so that congregants can drive older persons to worship services and social events. Many older persons are reluctant to ask for such assistance, but when it is offered, accept it gratefully. Such a ministry of transportation may mean the difference between one person feeling alienated, missing worship and congregational fellowship, and another person feeling connected to friends and the church.

All congregants could benefit from educational sessions about the challenges faced by older persons, and the congregation could offer such a session or could look into existing educational sessions in its own community. Such a session must be conducted by someone knowledgeable both in the challenges faced by older persons and in the community resources available. Many attendees will have their own set of issues: ill relatives with whom they share their homes and the problems inherent in that arrangement; lack of transportation for older persons to get to doctors' appointments or to the store; lack of social opportunities for older persons; and so forth. Thus the speaker must be quite knowledgeable about a whole host of issues and be able to offer practical solutions.

The pastor might consider taping his or her sermons for those older persons who cannot get to church. At a minimum, older parishioners who are homebound should be sent a church bulletin so they can keep up with the life of the church. Periodically, worship services could be conducted with older persons in mind; certain readings could be selected that honor older persons and hymns chosen with which older persons are familiar. After such a service, there could be a social event in which younger members of the congregation serve the older ones.

A congregation should encourage formation of a senior group from within its own membership as well as joining with older citizens from other congregations and the larger community. Social events aimed at older persons are another way to provide friendship, especially if transportation can be provided to those who want to attend. A pastor should make every effort to attend these social events. One could argue that a pastor has a great deal to do without attending social events. Yet it *is* important for a pastor to be involved with social events for older congregants for the same reason that he visits older persons at their homes or in nursing homes: to maintain contact with them, to show gratitude for the many years of support and service that they have already given their congregation, and to mirror Jesus to those who may feel forgotten by their church.

Finally, the congregation should not only look after its own elderly; it should also reach out to older persons in the community. If there is a nursing home close to the church, congregants can visit some of the persons living there, especially those who have few visitors. Especially welcome would be families who are willing to make visits. For many older persons, young children and pets bring a smile to their faces. Of more importance, visiting nursing homes teaches children something about being older in our society and the places in which some older persons must live when they are ill or alone. It also demonstrates to children the importance that their own parents place on honoring older persons—a concern so important that they plan a family outing to visit persons to whom they are not even related by blood, but to whom they are related by the Spirit. Such parental attitudes and behavior teach children more about our responsibilities to each other and the real meaning of the body of Christ than a year's worth of classroom lectures.

REFERENCES

Bronfenbrenner, U., McClelland, P., Wethington, E., et al. *The State of Americans.* New York: The Free Press, 1996.

STATISTICS

National Center for Health Statistics

www.cdc.gov/nchs/fastats/elderly.htm

Census

http://eire.census.gov/popest/archives/national/nation2/intfile2-1.txt

FOR MORE INFORMATION

Check local telephone listings under "elderly," "elder," "aged—services for," "retired," "senior citizens," and "support groups."

National Toll-Free Numbers

| AARP | 1-800-424-3410 |
| AARP Pharmacy Services | 1-800-456-2277 |

LOCAL RESOURCES

_____

_____

_____

_____

_____

Chapter 9

Substitute Care/Latchkey Children

*I*t is another difficult morning for Jeanette. Since her husband left her, she has had to return to work. Unfortunately, that meant that Jeremy had to be placed in a child-care center. Every morning, Jeanette must rise at 5:00 A.M. to get herself and Jeremy ready for the day. Jeremy does not like getting up so early and cries throughout breakfast and the drive to the child-care center. Once there, he screams when Jeanette is preparing to leave. Every morning Jeanette returns to her car, close to tears and badly shaken. Why can't life be the way it used to be?

Brenda is eight years old and home alone again. To make ends meet, both of Brenda's parents work outside the home. Because there are no after-school centers conveniently located to Brenda's home or school, her parents have decided that they would rather have her safe at home than traveling to a program. "My little girl is so mature," her father brags. "She can handle it." Brenda tries, but sometimes she gets so lonely and so afraid—especially when she has a hard day at school, or she hears noises outside. But she tries to be as brave as her father believes her to be because she doesn't want to worry him.

Physical Challenges

Children in child care may experience an increased number of infections, especially in their first year of attendance. Because certain infections make it impossible for a child safely to attend child care, parents might miss more days from work than they would have if their children were in home care. In general, the greater number of children grouped together, especially if they are younger than three years of age, the more likely infections are to spread

Facts to Consider

1. In 1997, the primary child-care arrangements of the ten million preschoolers with employed mothers were: 26 percent other relative care; 22 percent own parents at work; 22 percent nonrelatives (half in family day-care arrangements); 22 percent in organized facilities (3/4 in child-care centers) (Child Care Action Campaign). These percentages can vary by state.

2. Between five and seven million latchkey children go home to an empty house after school; roughly 35 percent of 12-year-olds are alone while their parents work (Campaign for Our Children). Approximately 12 percent of children aged 5 through 12 years stayed home alone as did over 40 percent of children aged 12 through 14.

3. A survey of working mothers in New York City revealed that 9 percent left their children alone regularly and 10 percent occasionally. Children were first left alone at a mean age of 9.8 years; 25 percent had been latchkey children since seven years of age and 10 percent since three years of age. By age 12, 95 percent of the children were in self-care. Of these, 75 percent of the children were left alone 1–3 hours/day, and 20 percent were left alone 4–8 hours/day (Fosarelli 173–74).

4. The number of children cared for by older siblings before and after school is unknown, but probably is in the millions.

throughout the class. This occurs because young children are unaware of certain hygienic practices (such as washing one's hands) to prevent the spread of germs. Caregivers who fail to wash their hands or clean soiled surfaces after helping children toilet or after changing diapers contribute to the spread of germs. Furthermore, young children must meet certain germs at least once before they are immune to them, and young children haven't met very many germs in the first year or so of life. Naturally, infections contracted in child care can then be brought home to the parents and other siblings, perhaps necessitating even more loss of time from work. Some employers are quite insensitive to parents missing work because of a child's illness; this insensitivity leads to additional parental stress.

Parental stress may also be present if the family must rise very early in order to get all members to their destinations on time. Rush-hour commuting time will be increased, as parents struggle to get a child to a child-care arrangement on time and themselves to work on time. When there is a traffic tie-up, the commute time will be even longer, thereby leading to additional stress. Furthermore, child care is expensive and may place a great financial burden on a family already strapped for funds.

School-age child care may also be an expensive item in a family's budget. In addition, a parent may worry about the school-age child who must travel alone on public transportation to an after-school program. Children who are home alone are also exposed to physical risks if their homes are unsafe. For example, easy access to matches, guns, knives, or cigarettes may lead to disaster. In addition, a child's lack of preparedness in the face of a physical crisis (e.g., electrical outage, toilet overflow, an attempted break-in) may also lead to tragedy. Physical manifestations of stress may also be found in the parents, especially if they are experiencing guilt or conflict over their child's child-care arrangement or ability to stay alone.

Emotional Challenges

Children may be cranky if they must get up earlier than usual to get to child care so that the parent can get to work on time. Although some children adjust quite well to this arrangement, others have a much more difficult time.

Children in child care have a number of predictable responses. Initially, most young children are understandably reluctant to leave their parents to be in the care of persons whom they do not know as well for most of their waking hours. Hence, there may be much crying at leave times as the child struggles to keep the parent with her. Paradoxically, on a parent's return later in the day, a child may sullenly ignore his parent or continue to play, crying only when his parent insists that it is time to leave.

Most children have an initial period of adjustment of several weeks before they settle down in the daily routine of child care. After this initial adjustment period, parents should beware if a child who was previously perfectly happy at child care suddenly becomes resistant to going, either by outright refusal or by crying or acting-out behavior. Perhaps there are problems at the child-care facility that the child wants to avoid. These may be minor, such as another child who doesn't like her, or can be more serious, such as abuse (physical, emotional, or sexual) by an adult at the facility. However, it should be emphasized that *abuse in child-care settings is far less common than abuse in children's own homes.* Another reason for a previously happy child to resist going to child care may be fear of leaving the parent because of a parent's recent illness, parental marital discord, the child's own illness, and so forth. In any event, a marked change in the child's behavior should always be taken seriously.

Parents, too, have their responses to child care. It is hard for parents to leave their "baby" in the care of nonrelatives for a substantial part of the day. Parents may become weepy or irritable depending on their coping styles. Parents may disagree with one another about placing a child in child care in the first place and in the particular child-care arrangement in particular. For some families, the more difficulty that a child has, the greater the conflict between the parents and, perhaps, the grandparents or other relatives and the parents. Failure to minimize parental disagreement in front of the child in question only makes adjustment more difficult for all concerned.

Parental discomfort at the thought of leaving a child in self-care is also not minimal. Although some parents do leave their children alone seemingly without a second thought, most parents feel uncomfortable. Many parents would not leave their child alone if there were other reasonable options. But, because of the lack of affordable, conveniently located after-school programs and the parental need to work, which is especially great in single-parent families, parents may have no other options. Parents ask themselves many questions: "Will my child be safe alone?" "Will he know what to do if someone tries to break in? If a fire breaks out? If he gets sick?" Safety concerns will be heightened if the child lives in an unsafe neighborhood or if the neighborhood has had a recent rash of crimes. Parents have legitimate concerns when their child is of a fearful temperament; they worry about the stress the child will experience by being home alone.

Other parents have good reason to be concerned because their children are risk-takers, willing to try anything once. When such children are home alone, parents may have legitimate fears about their child's safety and their property. Risk-taking children who are home alone may become involved in illegal activities, learn harmful information from the Internet, experiment in drugs or sex, play havoc with family property, or leave home to hang out at the mall or on street corners. In such cases, it is better for these children never to be left alone.

Many older children balk at attending after-school programs because they feel that they are mature enough to be on their own and because they may view after-school programs as "for babies." Sometimes a child is the best judge of her ability to stay home alone, but such beliefs can precipitate arguments between parents and child. Parents who know their children to be risk-takers may be especially reluctant to leave them home alone and may insist on after-school program attendance. So might parents who know that siblings will fight incessantly if they are home without parental supervision.

Depending on the age of the child, the safety of her neighborhood, and the support of her parents, the experience of being in self-care before and after school may be very positive or very negative. Children who are reasonably healthy, who live in safe neighborhoods, and who have the support of loving parents and caring neighbors generally do well in self-care after the age of ten years, although many jurisdictions set the legal lower age limit of self-care at twelve years. Children who are in self-care before they are ready to do so, live in crime-ridden neighborhoods, or lack the support of trusted adults, may experience the effects of stress such as chronic headaches, abdominal pains, or other nondescript complaints. Invariably, when these children are examined by a health professional, they seem to be in good health, and no physical cause is found for the complaints.

Being home alone when ill is especially worrisome for many children; a minor illness of childhood might grow in seriousness in the mind of a child who is alone and afraid. Such children want to be brave for their parents, but just may not be able to do so. Sometimes parents may really think that their child is doing well because he puts on a happy face and a brave front for his parents' benefit. Other children are far more direct, accusing parents of not loving them or preferring their jobs to them because the parents leave them alone. In either case, parental guilt may be marked. This is especially true for single parents who may have no other option but to work.

A word should be mentioned here about children in sibling-care. Older siblings may be called upon to care for younger ones before and after school. The older sibling may feel resentment because she must spend time caring for a younger sister or brother; in the older sibling's mind, the arrangement is not fair. From the younger sibling's point of view, the older sibling may act like a tyrant, bossing him around at whim. In either case, verbal disagreements with name calling may be common. In addition, there may be escalation to physical injury as one child strikes the other with a hand, fist, or other object. In some cases, sexual experimentation between siblings may occur, leading children to feel guilt and shame. *No* sexual activity among young children can be consensual, although sexual activity among adolescents might be. Sexual activity may be forced at any age.

Spiritual Challenges

From a parent's point of view, the spiritual challenge may lie in the fact that God has not helped them to make better provisions for their children. "Why won't God help us make more money so I won't have to work?" "Why won't God make my boss more sympathetic toward my needs?" "Why did God give me such a belligerent child who doesn't want to go to an after-school program and doesn't want to stay home alone?" "Why is my child such a terror when he stays home alone?" "Why doesn't God provide more child-care options near my home that I could afford?"

From a young child's point of view, the practice of a parent dropping him at child care may make him wonder whether God will leave him just like the parent does. Is God really at the child-care center, too? Suppose the child-care provider doesn't believe in God. Will God still be there? Similarly, when the child misbehaves at child care, he may wonder if God is angry at him. If he gets injured or becomes ill at child care, is it because God is punishing him? If his parent is late in coming, is the child being punished for his behavior during the day? Such magical thinking is typical of the thought processes of young children.

From the perspective of an older child who is left alone, her prayers might revolve around the arrangement, especially if she is afraid. God is invoked to protect the child in the parent's absence. Alternatively, the child may be angry at God for not making the family richer (so parents do not have to work or could live in a better neighborhood) or for giving her parents who seemingly prefer work to children. Some children begin to doubt that God cares for them at all.

Individual Responses

U.S. society is changing, and so is the way that we care for our youngest members. Although being home with a loving parent who does not work outside the home may be ideal, many parents do not have the option of staying home, and still other parents are far from loving. Hence, for many children, child care outside their homes is a reality, even while their parents agonize over the decision to use it. Both children and their parents need prayers.

Thus one can refrain from judging parents who use child-care arrangements as incompetent or uncaring. Persons whose own children are grown might be tempted to congratulate themselves that *they* did not leave their own children in someone else's care or home alone, but such self-congratulation is unhelpful. Times are very different now than they were thirty or forty years ago—or even twenty years ago.

Individuals can do several things to ease the way for children home alone after school. Adults who are home during the day can mark their houses with signs in a window as "safe havens" for home-alone children or those on their way home from school to come to in case of emergency. Granted, most parents will need to know an adult well before permitting their children to go to her house, but with so few adults home during the day, having a safe haven in the neighborhood can be a great relief to parents who are at work while their children are at home alone.

Adults who do not feel comfortable marking their houses with signs may be able to volunteer to be a "phone friend" to a child home alone. Such services are available in many communities. They are a source of relief for parents and also a friendly voice for children who are home alone. Again parents should be comfortable with *anyone* with whom their child has a relationship, even one conducted by telephone.

Congregational Responses

The congregation might consider starting a nursery during Sunday worship services so that parents can have a place for their young children *and* so that these children can learn to socialize with each other. They can also learn how to separate from their parents for a brief period, sure in the knowledge that their parents will return. During this time, children can play, nap, snack, and be taught to pray.

If there is sufficient need and interest, the congregation can develop its own before- and after-school program for children in its congregation and, perhaps, for children in the neighborhood. Of course, a disadvantage is that the congregation's children may not live in the neighborhood around the church and so may have to travel to get there. If the congregation operates a modest day-care center for younger children of working parents, an after-school program would not be difficult to add.

If it is impossible for the congregation to support such a center itself, it should be a strong voice for the development for such centers in its community, especially in school facilities or existing recreation centers. School facilities are ideal for such programs because children do not need to travel to them. The church should also strongly urge employers to be more children- and family-friendly, permitting parents to take leave time when their children are ill (which they will often be at younger ages) without fear of losing their jobs or incurring financial penalties. Advocating for the just treatment of parents and their families is a prophetic, Christ-like stance and demonstrates a congregation's willingness to imitate Jesus' own devotion to children.

REFERENCES

Fosarelli, P. "Latchkey Children." *Developmental and Behavioral Pediatrics* (1984), 5:173–77.

STATISTICS

Urban Institute
   http://newfederalism.urban.org/html/series_b/b7.html

Campaign for Our Children
   www.cfoc.org/5_educator/5_facts.cfm?Fact_ID=107

Child Care Action Campaign
  www.childcareaction.org/rfacts.html

FOR MORE INFORMATION

Check local telephone listings under "child care," "day care," "after-school care," "children's services," and "youth services."

LOCAL RESOURCES

_____

_____

_____

_____

_____

Chapter 10

Adolescent Sexuality and Pregnancy

Sixteen-year-old Dominique is an excellent student and has dreams of becoming a lawyer. But lately, her friends are teasing her about her "perfection" and her desire to maintain her virginity. Dominique is beginning to doubt that virginity is worth so much hassle.

Christine is pregnant and is very afraid. She is only fourteen years old and, although her eighteen-year-old boyfriend told her that he would love her forever, she hasn't seen him very much since she told him that she was pregnant. Chris is too afraid to tell anyone else because the news might get back to her folks. They have always been so strict that she is afraid that they will kill her when they find out.

Terrence has quite a reputation around town. Known as a "ladies man" at age 15, he estimates that he has had sex with over one hundred girls since he first became sexually active at age 12. He is proud of himself, even though he has had gonorrhea twice. "You play, you pay," he laughs.

Carlos is frightened. He thinks that he might be homosexual because, at fourteen years of age, he has no interest in girls. Because he is short and skinny, some of the guys in his school have already started rumors that he is gay, and they call him names. Carlos isn't attracted to males, but he keeps worrying, "Suppose those guys are right?"

❧❧❧❧❧❧❧

Physical Challenges

Adolescence is the time when a young person's body and feelings are changing so rapidly that he or she hardly can make sense of it all. One day he is

General Comments and Facts to Consider

Most adolescents are truly good people, trying to do as well as they can in school so that they can one day become responsible adults. However, for all adolescents, their bodies are changing so rapidly and their burgeoning sexuality is such a prominent part of their lives that issues of sexuality and the consequences of acting upon (or not acting upon) sexual drives is a major feature of this age group.

1. When asked if they had ever had sexual intercourse, 53 percent of students in grades 9–12 reported yes. Nationwide, 19 percent of students have had sexual intercourse with four or more partners in their lifetime; more males than females report this activity (National Center for Chronic Disease Prevention and Health Promotion).

2. By age 15, 24 percent of black females, 26 percent of white males and females, and 69 percent of black males have had sexual intercourse at least once; by age 19, 83 percent of black females, 76 percent of white females, 86 percent of white males, and 98 percent of black males have had intercourse at least once. For many adolescents, sexual activity is part of a complex of behaviors that include school problems (either disciplinary or scholastic), school suspension, truancy, runaway, fighting, and substance abuse, including alcohol and marijuana (Elster 1044).

3. Because many teens use no contraception or ineffective means of contraception, there are many teen pregnancies. Of the 35 million adolescents (defined as individuals between the ages of ten and nineteen years), each year about 10 percent of teenage girls in the United States—more than one million young women under age 20—become pregnant. Approximately 50 percent of these girls give birth (nearly 470,000 births to 15–19-year-olds, with 157,000 of these to 15–17-year-olds, according to the National Center for Health Statistics); 30–40 percent obtain an abortion; and the remainder have spontaneous miscarriages. The percentage of all nonmarital births in teens is approximately 65 percent (over 50 percent of births to all teenagers and 90 percent of births to black teenagers). Adolescents who are from minorities or who are poor are less likely to abort than are girls of higher socioeconomic status. Less than 5 percent of adolescent mothers put their babies up for adoption (Stevens-Simon 322). Children of the youngest adolescents do less well over time than do children of older adolescents or adult women (Hardy 802).

4. Every year three million teens acquire a sexually transmitted disease. Both chlamydia and gonorrhea are more common among teens than among older men and women (Alan Guttmacher Institute).

strong, the next day he is tripping all over himself. One day she is mature, the next day she is crying, asking for her mother to hold her hand. One day he has all the girls around him; the next day, girls shun him. One day she has lots of friends, the next day no one will sit with her at lunch. The rapid increase in height makes some adolescents physically awkward. The surge of hormones makes acne more likely, leading to embarrassment. The upsurge of hormones can also produce sexual feelings toward the opposite sex that are played out in physical reactions. Changes in both hormones and the size of the larynx makes the pitch of a boy's voice very unpredictable.

Sexual activity is not always welcomed. Sometimes adolescents have sex because "everyone is doing it" and not because they want to do so. Some adolescents have had sex so that fellow classmates will not ridicule them as "babies" or "queers." These names are painful for all to whom they are directed, but are particularly so for adolescents who are slow to develop physically. In fact, they *do* look much younger or, in the case of boys, less "manly." Some girls run from their developing adult bodies by starving themselves, believing themselves to be too fat. As they lose more and more weight, their menstrual periods cease, and their bodies again take on the appearance of that of a child.

Having sex *is* fraught with problems. Sexually transmitted diseases are on the rise, especially in adolescents who take risks by engaging in unprotected sex because of their feeling of invulnerability ("it'll never happen to me"). Pregnancy is a real possibility. Because an adolescent girl may deny her condition far into her pregnancy, she is less likely to eat properly, take vitamins, exercise regularly and safely, and receive adequate prenatal care, all of which contribute to an infant's well-being. For these reasons, adolescents have more problems with pregnancy and give birth to a greater number of low-birthweight infants than do other age groups. The pregnant adolescent will miss time from school and, indeed, may never return to school after the baby is born, thus setting herself and her child up for a life of poverty. Few adolescents give their infants up for adoption, even in the worst of situations.

Abortion is also not an easy answer for most adolescents. Although some adolescents view their fetus as an unwanted object and use repeated abortions as a means of birth control, many more adolescents see the fetus as a living being, and they believe abortion is wrong or dangerous. However, sometimes, in fear or at the insistence of their boyfriends, girls seek to put an end to their pregnancies. The guilt that many of these young women experience may be enormous, even years later.

Emotional Challenges

The roller-coaster spectrum of feelings in adolescence is difficult for both teenagers and their parents to manage. For parents, their previously well-behaved, happy child has become a young woman or man full of contradictions, hair-trigger mood changes, and attachment to peer pressure. Parents worry about the safety of their adolescents and are concerned that they make the best use of their gifts and talents. Adolescents, on their part, frequently want less of their parents, although sometimes they still want more. Parents have a difficult time knowing what mood a teen is likely to have on any given day; adolescents, themselves, do not always understand their moods. Battles over insignificant issues (such as clothing and makeup) and significant ones (such as curfews, drug use, sexual activity) are common. Patience and good humor are useful to work through these issues, but these may be in short supply.

At the one extreme, some adolescents may be so driven to perfection or so frightened by their sexual development that they develop eating disorders. Girls outnumber boys in this area, but boys *can* be affected. Anorexia (lack of appetite for food) and bulimia (actively purging oneself) have physical manifestations and deep psychological roots. Such persons are usually good students and are driven to perfection. When an anorexic girl sees her body, she sees it in a distorted way, sometimes because someone teased her about being "too fat." Taking it to heart, no matter how unrealistic such a comment was, she will proceed to lose weight. Not satisfied with a "normal" weight (which she now sees as still too fat), she continues to lose weight, sometimes to a dangerous degree. All the while, she cannot see that she is too skinny. Bribes to eat and scolding by worried parents usually are useless. Sexual behavior is nonexistent because boys do not want to date someone who looks like an undeveloped ten-year-old.

At the other extreme, other adolescents manifest bravado and a sense of invulnerability, both of which are deeply concerning to parents. When a person feels invulnerable, he may take risks because bad consequences will "never happen to me." Thus sexual activity, substance abuse, reckless driving, and illegal activities may be explored by the adolescent, sometimes with tragic consequences. Frequently these risks are taken with persons whom their parents don't know or of whom they do not approve.

Adolescents may feel the need to associate with teens or young adults whom their parents dislike. Some of this behavior may be the natural tendency of adolescents to choose their own identity (and hence their own friends) separate from that of their parents. In this attempt, adolescents may purposefully choose friends of whom their parents disapprove simply to upset their parents, or they may choose activities of which their parents disapprove. All of this is part of the adolescent struggle to establish a unique identity, separate from that of parents.

Sexual behavior on the part of adolescents is a further attempt to establish themselves independently from their parents. The reasoning is: "If I am old enough to give my body to someone else, then I am really an adult." Unfortunately, some adolescents may see free sexual behavior in their unmarried parents who permit their sexual partners to "sleep over." It will be difficult if not impossible for such parents to send a clear message to their children that sexual activity in adolescence is wrong. If the parent can do it, why can't the adolescent?

The issue of sexually transmitted diseases is also an emotional one. "What will people think of me if they know I've had gonorrhea?" "What would my boyfriend say if he knew I got chlamydia, but not from him?" In this era of HIV disease and herpes infections, there is also the possibility of contracting a sexually transmitted disease that cannot be cured and, in the case of HIV disease, may also take one's life. There is no such thing as safe sex; there is only safer sex, and most adolescents who are sexually active do not consistently practice it.

For the boyfriend of an adolescent girl who is pregnant, there may be real concern as to whether he is the father and whether he will have to support the baby. Most adolescents do not make enough money to support a child. For a girl who is pregnant, there is the fear of telling her family and friends and the possible ostracism that she may face. There is also the fear of the unknown: "What will this baby be like?" "Will I be a good mother?" "How will I support this baby?" "Will I ever be able to go back to school?" "Do I even want to be a mother?" If an adolescent girl decides to have an abortion, she may fear the procedure and the consequences. Yet sometimes she fears these less than telling her family that she is pregnant.

Once her baby is born, a young mother may resent the time demands that the infant places on her. After all, adolescence is supposed to be a time of freedom. How can a young mother be free? If she permits her own mother to care for the baby while she "runs," she risks losing her identity as the child's mother. Clashes between an infant's teenage mother and grandmother can occur over the proper raising of the child. An adolescent may consider running away with or without her baby.

Adolescents are also more likely to abuse their infants than are women in their twenties (see chapter 13) and, compared with other age groups, are more likely to become involved with substance abuse (see chapter 12) and to consider suicide as an option (see chapter 3). Adolescents are also more likely to become victims of date rape and physical/sexual abuse at the hands of their partners (see chapter 14).

The issue of sexual identity and orientation may come squarely to the fore in adolescence, as some young people learn that they are attracted to members of their own gender. The overwhelming sense of confusion, shame, guilt, and adjustment that is encountered is extremely difficult for adolescents to handle without assistance. Bad decisions can be made in haste or out of fear of their family's reaction.

Spiritual Challenges

Adolescence is the stage in which young people question the validity of their own religious traditions, and, sometimes, even the existence of God. Theodicy issues come to the fore. "How can God exist and permit small children to suffer or people to starve to death?" asks the adolescent in anguish. And, although these are not strictly adolescent questions, this is perhaps the first time in a young person's life that such questions have been raised. They are frightening to the adolescent. Who is in charge? Human beings? Well, they're certainly making a mess of things. God? Well, where is God in the midst of all this? Adolescents may also wonder how they can be sure that their family's religion is "right." After all, they see plenty of people from different faith traditions who are as good as they are—or even better. Even some people who don't attend church at all seem to be very good people. So why is church necessary? This phase is a necessary part of becoming one's own person with one's own beliefs—not just because they are their parents' beliefs.

When bad things happen to the adolescent, such as a sexually transmitted disease, a pregnancy, addiction, abuse, or violence, she may ask, "Why me?" She may wonder if God is punishing her for some deed or is testing her. Frequently, this will lead the adolescent to fear God, to discount God's influence in her life, or to deny God's existence altogether.

Parents, too, may wonder where God is when their cooperative children turn into persons with their own minds, which are frequently opposed to the parental mind. They may wonder if they have made a fundamental mistake as they watch with horror as their children reject the family faith or traditions. They worry as their children mix with the wrong friends or get involved with activities of which the parents disapprove. They may ask, "Where are you, God?" or wonder if God is punishing them for their own misdeeds as adolescents. Their faith, too, may be shaken.

Individual Responses

Many individuals, especially those without adolescents in their families, believe the media's portrayal of adolescents: they are all sexually active, ready to commit crimes, use drugs and alcohol, and are disrespectful of adults and authority. Knowledgeable adults as well as adolescents themselves need to correct this impression. Although many adolescents have these problems, the majority of adolescents are good people, eager for the guidance of their parents and other trusted adults. Adults are called to seek and welcome opportunities to work with adolescents.

Parents can use all the prayers they can get from others so that they will be able, with their teens, to weather the adolescent years. Parents need wisdom in discerning when their child is in trouble—physically, emotionally, and spiritually—*and* need to recognize when one of their children is "too" perfect, "too" thin, "too" rebellious, or "too" different. Sometimes it takes the insights of friends or teachers to point this out to the parents in a spirit of love. Parents must be able to be open to the insights of trusted others and act upon those insights, just as they would act upon their own insights. In addition, wise parents (or teachers or pastors) are not threatened by adolescent questions (or grumblings) about their faith tradition or about God's role in the world; instead, they welcome and encourage dialogue with young people.

Congregational Responses

Individuals can learn how good adolescents are when congregations permit adolescents to take a role in worship, organize charity events, teach younger children, and help in the church office. Many adolescents long to be really needed by their congregation, to be given *real* work, not just busy work. Leaders of the congregation can think creatively and assure that this can happen.

Adolescents need their own group within the congregation within which they can socialize and use as a forum to discuss the important issues in their lives and how Jesus would respond in thorny situations. They need to know what their church teaches about certain issues and how their church will support them as they attempt to form good consciences. Obviously, this adolescent group must be led by someone who is gifted in working with young people, able to listen creatively and lead as necessary.

Congregations can set up a parenting session for the parents of adolescents that reviews the normal stages of adolescence, frequent areas of disagreement between teens and parents, and ways to minimize conflict. This type of session should be presented by someone with lived experience in working with adolescents. Sometimes, parents of adolescents will form themselves into a support group. The pastoral staff should also collect information on available services for adolescents in their community so that they can share it with congregants.

A pastor can address adolescents periodically, helping them understand why their church holds the views it does about sex in adolescence, abortion, substance abuse, and other issues. Adolescents need the chance to ask questions and to debate adult opinions before they can truly accept what they are being told. If a pastor does not feel well equipped to talk with adolescents, another leader in the church can do so. But it should never be the opinion of a congregation that it has no responsibilities in discussing these matters with its young members because "it's up to the parents to do so." To be the church means to be in community, and to be in community means to share responsibility for sharing information.

Being in community also means to pray and care for each other. When an adolescent member of the congregation becomes pregnant or discovers he is gay, the congregation as a whole must be supportive of the young person. Condemnation was not Jesus' way; he said, "Let him without sin cast the first stone." After all, which adults have made no mistakes in their own youth? The affected adolescent is going through a crisis; so is his family. A pastor can show by example what it means to be present with someone in difficult times—not nosily inquiring about details but instead offering to help in whatever way the family or adolescent finds most helpful. Sometimes that will mean listening; sometimes it will mean wiping tears. Sometimes it will mean dispelling rumors or educating rumormongers or the uninformed about the facts. Always it will mean acting Christ-like: teaching when there is ignorance; offering support when there is none; loving when there is rejection.

REFERENCES

Bidwell, R., and Deisher, R. "Adolescent Sexuality." *Pediatric Annals* (1991), 20:293–302.

Brooks-Gunn, J., and Chase-Lansdale, L. "Children Having Children: Effects on the Family System." *Pediatric Annals* (1991), 20:467–81.

Elster, A., Ketterlinus, R., and Lamb, M. "Association between Parenthood and Problem Behavior in a National Sample of Adolescents." *Pediatrics* (1990), 85:1044–50.

Hardy, J., Shapiro, S., Astone, N., et al. "Adolescent Childbearing Revisited." *Pediatrics* (1997), 100:802–9.

Jaskiewicz, J., and McAnarney, E. "Pregnancy during Adolescence." *Pediatrics in Review* (1994), 15:32–38.

Stevens-Simon, C., and White, M. "Adolescent Pregnancy." *Pediatric Annals* (1991), 20:322–31.

STATISTICS

National Center for Health Statistics

www.childstats.gov/ac2002/indicators.asp?IID=31&id+4

www.cdc.gov/nchs/releases/02news/womenbirths.htm
www.cdc.gov/nchs/fastats/teenbrth.htm
www.cdc.gov/nccdphp/dash/publications/ahson1994/summary.htm

Alan Guttmacher Institute

www.agi-usa.org/pubs/fb_teen_sex.html

FOR MORE INFORMATION

Check local telephone listings under "teen/youth/adolescent organizations/ services" (private and government), and "Health Department—sexually transmitted diseases division."

National Toll-Free Number

CDC Hotline for STD/AIDS   1-800-342-2437

LOCAL RESOURCES

_____

_____

_____

_____

_____

Chapter 11

Educational Failure, Poverty, Homelessness, Hunger, and Unemployment

*T*abitha and her baby brother are spending another night in a shelter with their mother, who was evicted from her apartment. Although she is four, Tabitha looks more like a two-year-old with scrawny arms and legs; her nine-month-old brother cannot sit up yet and has had one ear infection after another. Tabitha's mother never finished high school and works at entry-level jobs that pay only a minimum wage. Because of her lack of education and her lack of skills, she is pessimistic as to whether she can ever do any better for herself or her children. This is the third apartment her family has had to leave—all because she cannot pay her rent on time with her meager salary.

~~~~~~~~

Physical Challenges

The physical challenges of chronic hunger, homelessness, and poverty are intellectually easier to understand than they are to comprehend emotionally. Every person has been hungry at some time or another; imagine if that hunger pain was chronic and unremitting. Every person has been short of a few dollars at a store at one time or another; imagine if that were the norm rather than the exception. Nearly every person has run short of money before the next pay period at one time or another; imagine if that happened regularly and deeply.

In this country, being a poor adult means that one is a second-class citizen who isn't adult enough to handle his financial affairs properly. Even if a parent works two entry-level jobs but his family is still poor, such a parent will be made to feel like a failure. Lack of proper education or training accounts for an overdependence on entry-level positions that some persons have. With an educational system that promotes students to the next grade for social reasons, whether or not they can do the grade-appropriate work, there will continue to be persons who are relegated to a lifetime of entry-level jobs.

Children who are chronically poor and hungry have a number of physical problems related to deficiencies in essential nutrients. They are generally too thin because of a lack of fat tissue. In addition, their teeth are in poor repair. Depending on how hungry they are, they may be cranky or sleepy. If they are chronically malnourished, their attention spans may be limited. Such children tend to do poorly in school, making underachievement a strong likelihood. Children without a regular place to live may have to live in shelters, on the streets, or wherever their parents can find. Such places may not be physically safe from violence or crime. In addition, such temporary domiciles may not be safe from lead. Lead poisoning is particularly detrimental to young children. A high burden of lead can cause a number of physical problems, such as abdominal pain and seizures. A high lead burden may also affect the ability of a young child to learn and process information, leading to learning disabilities. This, too, leads to school failure.

Children living in shelters may be subject to more infections because of the increased number of people present who may have infections or infestations with lice or scabies. Chronic colds and ear infections are associated with an increased likelihood of hearing deficit, which, in turn, is associated with an increased likelihood of learning problems.

Emotional Challenges

Children who are chronically poor, hungry, and homeless share one attribute: they tend to feel badly about themselves because society discounts them and their families. They may be expected to do poorly in school or to behave badly. They believe that they are "not as good" as other children, that they do not "deserve" what other children deserve. Their schools frequently mirror this belief. Halls littered with trash, dirty/smelly bathrooms, playgrounds littered with syringes and needles, and demoralized teachers in such settings speak loudly to poor children that they do not deserve better. The same message may be imparted by their parents, who have internalized that message since their own childhood.

Hence, these children can learn to hate themselves and to hate those who look down on them. This is especially true if these children are less gifted academically and are ridiculed by their brighter classmates. Such ridicule will make it almost a certainty that they will drop out or fail. Without a decent education *and* adults in their lives who encourage them to stay in school and to

General Comments and Facts to Consider

The following problems are grouped together because they are all closely related.

1. Poverty
The definition of poverty is based on the amount of income needed to maintain a *minimally* healthy diet.

In 2002, the poverty level was defined as a yearly income of $18,307 for a family of four persons. This amount of money must cover food, rent, clothing, health needs, and miscellaneous items. In the United States, 16 percent of children are growing up in poverty (U.S. Census Bureau).

There are several myths about the poor:

- The poor do not want to work or are lazy.
- Most of the poor are minorities.
- Most of the poor cheat the welfare system.
- Once a person is poor, he or she will always be poor.

The facts are quite different:

- An hourly wage of $6.50 means $13,000 per annum, which is below the poverty line for a family of four. Most poor people do work, but because of health limitations or educational limitations, they cannot earn more than the minimum wage.
- Two-thirds of the poor are whites, although minorities are more likely to be poor relative to their proportion in the population.
- In no state does the combination of food stamps and Aid to Families with Dependent Children (AFDC) payments raise a family up to the official poverty level.
- Only half of the poor are persistently poor; the rest have one or two bad years, usually as a result of unemployment. Most welfare recipients do not come from welfare families.
- Women are the majority of minimum wage earners. Therefore, female-headed households are more likely to be poor than male-headed ones. If a woman was working a minimum wage job in 1995, she would have been earning $4.25/hour (= $8,840/year). There has been a sharp increase in the number of female-headed households due to the high divorce rate and the number of unmarried adolescents and women having children (Byrd 654–55).

2. Unemployment
In late 2002, the unemployment rate varied, by state, from a low of 3.7 percent to a high of 7.0 percent; the overall average for the nation was around 5 percent (U.S. Department of Labor). Some factors that make it likely that someone will be poor include unemployment, underemployment, and school failure or dropout. Although more whites are unemployed than are blacks or Hispanics, the percentages of unemployment for the latter are much higher than for whites (10 percent vs. 5 percent). Underemployment denotes a lower level of work than that for which one is qualified or fewer hours worked per week than one would prefer. Layoffs and downsizing are major reasons for unemployment, but the most important cause is school failure or dropping out (Byrd 654–55).

3. School failure
    A. Ten to fifteen percent of the school-age population receives some form of specialized educational assistance (McInerny 325). Since 1970, the proportion of U.S. students between the

ages of 6–8 years who are older than their same-grade peers has doubled (11 percent in 1971 to 22 percent in 1990). The proportion of adolescents who are old-for-grade has increased from 23 percent in 1971 to 32 percent in 1993. Old-for-grade is more common for males, blacks, Hispanics, children from single-parent households, poor children, students for whom English is a second language, and those with mothers with low educational achievement. Both old-for-grade and retention are associated with behavior problems (Byrd 654–55). As of 2000, one in four eighth-graders scored below basic levels in reading, 48 percent below basic math, and 40 percent below basic science (U.S. Department of Education).

B. Over the last decade, between 347,000 and 544,000 10th–12th graders left school each year without successfully completing a high-school program (National Center for Education Statistics). Dropout rates are high for African Americans and Hispanics because of their alienation from a Caucasian-run system, lack of role models, teenage pregnancy, and their greater likelihood to be labeled (rightly or wrongly) as "troublemakers" and, hence, encouraged to drop out.

C. Failure to finish school is associated with illiteracy. Fifteen percent of urban high school *graduates* read below the sixth-grade level, and 26 percent of adults cannot determine if their paychecks are correct. Urban minority youths show the greatest levels of illiteracy, which translates into an inability to secure a decent wage, itself a predictor of future poverty (Byrd 654–55). Forty million adult U.S. citizens are functionally illiterate, meaning they cannot read and write well enough to fill out a job application, maintain a checking account, or read a book to a child. Such individuals are more likely to be chronically unemployed and dependent on public assistance. Today, 63 percent of persons with low literacy skills receive welfare benefits for over five years (Literacy Volunteers of America).

4. Hunger

Being poor means that one is likely to be in poor health, have poor nutritional status, or have unstable living conditions. On any given day in the United States, thirty-three million people, including thirteen million children, live in households that experience hunger (3 percent of all households) or the risk of hunger (7 percent of all households). Hunger affects four million low-income children younger than twelve years of age in the United States, and nearly an additional ten million children are at risk. In 1985, twenty-five million U.S. citizens were hungry; in 1991, that had increased to thirty million and is still increasing. Hunger and malnutrition are associated with an increased likelihood of adverse health, school problems, and a higher mortality rate (Cutts 489).

5. Homelessness

A. Each year, 2.5–3 million people lack access to a conventional residence. On any given day in the United States, 500,000–1,000,000 people are homeless. Only one-third of homeless persons are substance abusers.

B. Families with children account for 43 percent of the homeless population; the largest segment of homeless persons are families with children. On any given night, 100,000 children live in shelters, and 500,000 are homeless each year. The majority of these are younger than six years old (Bassuk 92).

C. Today, 100,000–300,000 adolescents are living on the streets, and 30–50 percent of the 220,000–280,000 U.S. homeless children do not attend school (A and C from Committee on Community Health Services 789–90).

work hard there, they will not be able to rise out of the poverty that ensnares their families. In many cases, their parents cannot assist their children with their schoolwork because they themselves failed academically.

Children who are chronically hungry feel badly about themselves, physically and emotionally, because they frequently are irritable or can't stay awake in class; they may be ridiculed by other students or teachers for being so "out of it." To feed their hunger, they may snack on junk foods loaded with high contents of sugar and salt. With a heavy dose of sugar, children's own blood sugars may roller-coaster, depending on what they have eaten and when; alternating mood swings are common. With a heavy dose of salt, their blood pressures may rise, potentially leading to health problems throughout their lives.

Children who are homeless are deeply embarrassed by their lack of a home and go to great lengths to hide their homelessness from teachers and other students. Children who live in shelters are often the brunt of cruel comments from some of their classmates who, although poor, at least have a house to which they can return each day after school.

Spiritual Challenges

"Why am I poor, God?" asks the young child. "What did I do to deserve this? Was I bad? Am I being punished? Why can't I live in a real house?" It is no surprise that children think that being hungry or poor is a punishment. After all, what do many parents do when their children misbehave? Send them to bed without dinner. Take away their allowances. And, when children hear adults criticizing poor people as lazy and unmotivated, either in day-to-day conversations or in the media, it is easy to see how children might think that God is punishing them or their parents for their laziness or lack of motivation. Tragically, they might also hear that message from church pulpits.

It is easy to understand how a child with chronic hunger or without a home could be angry with God for his situation. Hunger hurts—why should any child hurt? Why does God let this happen? Having no home one can call one's own is a real loss; why should any child lack a home? Doesn't God care? Without some physical support in the form of food or shelter, such children have little reason to believe in good people who worship a good God.

Similarly, when a child does poorly in school, she can blame God. "If God made me, how come he made me so dumb?" asked one girl sadly. "If God hears prayers and loves me, like my pastor says, why doesn't God let me do better in school when I pray so hard?" "If God really loves me, why does he let the other kids make fun of me?" Although such questions may seem simplistic to adults, they are weighty to the young child who struggles with them.

Without evidence of a God who acts through people taking an interest in him, a child may feel as if he is despised by peers, by adults, by society as a whole, and maybe even by God. "If God doesn't like me," asked a boy, "why did he bother making me? My mother says she wishes she never had me. Maybe I shouldn't have been born at all."

Without evidence that they are beloved of God, children who are on the lowest rungs of society may easily grow into adults who lack faith. On the other hand, if poor children are encouraged to pray and attend church, they may have a robust faith in both childhood and adulthood. This happens when a child is exposed to a person of faith who believes in the child's worth and demonstrates that belief through actions.

Individual Responses

What can individuals do about the poor, the hungry, or the homeless? It seems like such an overwhelming task! What can one person do?

One person can help *one other* person. It is not sufficient merely to throw money at a cause aimed at the poor, hungry, or homeless. To be sure, such causes need financial support so that they can assist as many persons as possible. But some people feel that writing a check abrogates them from any further responsibilities. Nothing could be further from the truth for people of faith. Is it possible to offer one's services, once a week or even once a month, to the local soup kitchen, outreach center, homeless shelter, or tutoring program? After all, in Jesus' parable of the Good Samaritan, the Samaritan did not just pay for the lodging of the injured Jew at the inn. He became involved. He lifted him upon his animal and carried him to the inn. If we are reluctant to become involved, we must ask ourselves why. If we say we have insufficient time, do we have time to do other activities (such as watching television) that are not essential? If we say that we are afraid of certain people, what does that say about our own inner prejudices? That all poor people are violent, lazy, or dirty? Do we fear that we won't be appreciated for our good works, because the last time we tried to help a homeless person, he cursed at us and rejected our attempts? What is the reason we help others in the first place? For ourselves? For the person in need? Or for God so that God's reign may come to pass here on earth? Our own attitudes must be carefully examined if we strongly prefer to help the poor "at arm's length." In addition to praying for those less fortunate than ourselves, we are also called to pray for the conversion of our own attitudes toward them, praying that Jesus' attitude toward the poor becomes our own.

Individuals with children can bring them along to such ministering efforts, teaching them, by example, how Jesus would want us to treat our sisters and brothers. Being with the poor, the homeless, and the hungry teaches children that these people indeed are siblings in God's family; they are not "those other people." It teaches children that we are all connected in some way, and when someone is hurting, those who are not hurting can help relieve the pain. It also teaches children that, when one person is diminished and others stand by, doing nothing to assist that person or to be in solidarity with her, we are all diminished as well.

Children, too, can explore their own feelings about the poor, homeless, and hungry, especially any images that they may have received from the media. Children can be helped to understand that most poor people are not criminals or addicts, but are simply poor. They can be reminded that many children are poor—not because they did anything wrong but because they were born into a poor family. Children can be asked what *they* would like to do to help poor children in their own communities. Adults can remind children to keep those who are poor in their prayers; adults best model this behavior by praying for God's poor—wherever they may live—publicly with the children.

Congregational Responses

The congregation can offer wonderful ways to encourage children to get involved with others less fortunate than themselves. Perhaps one congregation could partner with a poorer congregation, not only at holiday times but throughout the year. Children from the poorer congregation can be asked both what they would want the more affluent children to do with them and for them, and also what they, the poorer children, would like to do with and for the affluent children. Let the poor guide the children's ministries to the poor. Similarly, the adult poor could be asked what other adults can do to help them. After all, it is arrogant to assume that we know what the poor need, unless we ourselves are poor. Far better is it to take Jesus for our example. The Gospels relate that before he healed someone in need, Jesus frequently asked, "What would you have me do for you?" What a gracious way of relating to people! If Jesus, in all his wisdom, could place himself at the requests of others, should we not do the same?

Naturally, during holidays a congregation may want to prepare food baskets or procure toys for the less fortunate in their neighborhood. But it is important to ask what is needed or desired before making assumptions. Even if the poor family is in the congregation itself, it is far better to ask what parents need or what toys the children would like rather than "surprising" them with items that might not be useful.

Perhaps the congregation could open its own outreach center or soup kitchen staffed by congregants, if the need is great enough in its community. Alternatively, the congregation could formally join with existing services in the community, taking its own turn serving at the shelter, soup kitchen, or outreach center. Members of the pastoral team, especially the pastor, should be part of the congregation who serve in this way. Their service is a fine example to the rest of the congregation of the type of servant leadership that Jesus so clearly embodied. In addition, it will make a greater impression upon the congregation when the pastor preaches about wealth and materialism, if congregants know that *their* pastor is willing to give up some of his own comfort to become personally involved with those whom society has ignored. For, if church leadership is involved, what excuse can a congregant seriously make not to become involved as well? Pastors who join in this effort can make a lasting impression on their congregations, especially the children. For their words are not just the words of one who has higher theological education, but are the words of one who has heard Jesus' call and has responded. That is Jesus' challenge to us all.

Pastors have unique opportunities to preach on poverty, urging congregants to examine their own prejudices, whether outward or inward. Such preaching is in the tradition of the great prophets of Israel. It consists in challenging the mind-sets of those who might prefer to remain in a comfort zone, insulated from life's seamier aspects. This may make both congregants and pastor uncomfortable. But Christianity is not a faith tradition of comfort if it is to remain true to the one for whom it is named. How did Jesus show his solidarity with the poor of his day? Was he not homeless himself? Did he not feed the hungry? Did he not have compassion for the masses? Did he not pray for them? In good conscience, how can we do less?

REFERENCES

Bassuk, E., Weinreb, L., Dawson, R., et al. "Determinants of Behavior in Homeless and Low Income Housed Preschool Children." *Pediatrics* (1997), 100:92–100.

Byrd, R., Weitzman, M., and Auinger, P. "Increased Behavior Problems Associated with Delayed School Entry and Delayed School Progress." *Pediatrics* (1997), 100:654–61.

Committee on Community Health Services. "Health Needs of Homeless Children and Families." *Pediatrics* (1996), 98:789–91.

Cutts, D., Pheley, D., and Geppert, J. "Hunger in Midwestern Inner-City Young Children." *Archives of Pediatric and Adolescent Medicine* (1998), 152:489–93.

Hahn, B. "Children's Health: Racial and Ethnic Differences in the Use of Prescription Medicines." *Pediatrics* (1995), 95:727–32.

McInerny, T. "Children Who Have Difficulty in School: A Primary Pediatrician's Approach." *Pediatrics in Review* (1995), 16:325–32.

Wood, D., Valdez, B. C., Hayashi, T., et al. "Health of Homeless Children and Housed, Poor Children." *Pediatrics* (1990), 86:858–66.

STATISTICS

Poverty—Census Information

www.census.gov/hhes/poverty/poverty01/pov01hi.html
www.census.gov/hhes/poverty/threshld/thresh02.html

Unemployment—Bureau of Labor Statistics

www.bls.gov/lau/home.htm

School Failure, Dropout, Illiteracy—Department of Education

www.ed.gov/offices/OVAE/HS/studentrisk.html
http://nces.ed.gov/pubs2002/droppub_2001/
www.lvanca.org/getinvolved/factsheet.html

Hunger—Bread for the World

www.bread.org/hungerbasics/domestic.html

Homelessness—HUD

www.huduser.org/publications/homeless/homelessness/ch_2b.html
www.huduser.org/publication/homeless/homelessness/ch_2b2.html

FOR MORE INFORMATION

Check local telephone listings (private and government) under "education," "special education," "employment," "housing," "volunteer opportunities," "food stamps/supplements," "Salvation Army," "homeless shelters."

LOCAL RESOURCES

_____

_____

_____

_____

Chapter 12

Substance Abuse and Depression

*T*en-year-old Barry has learned to get high on airplane glue. He really likes the way it makes him feel. His thirteen-year-old friend Robert has promised to show him some other ways to get high.

Melanee got drunk again. She spent the night at her friend's house with her parents' permission but lied to them when she told them that her friend's parents would be home. There were no adults present, and the kids had a pretty wild time; after six beers, fourteen-year-old Melanee passed out. When she woke up, she found an older boy sleeping next to her. She doesn't know how he got there. She hopes nothing "happened."

Anthony is hooked on cocaine and has been for eighteen months. At age 16, he is doing poorly in school and wants to drop out, but his parents are against it. He needs money for his habit, so he works after school and on weekends. His parents wonder aloud where all his money goes.

Physical Challenges

The physical effects of drugs and alcohol vary by the substance used. Alcohol can, in small doses, calm and relax a person, but in higher doses can cause agitation or violent behavior. Amphetamines can cause a sense of euphoria and a "take charge" mentality, but can also cause a person to spin out of control. Barbiturates can help a person to sleep, but can also cause extreme drowsiness and interfere with normal daily functions. Marijuana can cause relaxation, but can also cause problems with memory and rational thinking. Cocaine can give one a high, but can also cause one to act irrationally and

89

General Comments and Facts to Consider

We live in a society that gives a clear message that one should always feel good and that one may attain that state any way one can.

1. One of these ways is by the use of alcohol. Nearly eleven million men and five million women abuse alcohol or are dependent on it (National Institute of Alcohol Abuse & Alcoholism). Over ten million persons aged 12–20 years report current alcohol use, that is, they are underage drinkers (Office of Applied Studies, Substance Abuse and Mental Health Statistics). In addition, 29 percent of adolescents reported having had their first significant drink before thirteen years of age (National Institute of Alcohol Abuse and Alcoholism).

2. According to 1994 statistics, over 90 percent of all teenagers have experimented with alcohol; 65 percent have used alcohol in the past month. Drinking at least once a day is reported by 5 percent of high school seniors. In addition, 67 percent of eighth-graders, 81 percent of tenth-graders, and 87 percent of twelfth-graders have experimented with alcohol. Fourteen teenagers die in alcohol-related accidents each day, while three hundred are injured (Takahashi 39).

3. Binge drinking is also on the rise. Binge drinking is defined as taking five or more drinks in a row at least once in the previous two weeks. Fourteen percent of eighth-graders, 23 percent of tenth-graders, 28 percent of twelfth-graders, and 40 percent of college students self-report binge drinking (Takahashi 39).

4. There were over 19,000 alcohol-induced deaths in 2000, not including motor vehicle deaths (National Center for Health Statistics). Between 50–65 percent of people who die in fires have blood alcohol levels indicating intoxication (National Council on Alcoholism and Drug Dependence).

5. Nearly six million citizens of the United States have drug problems (National Council on Alcoholism and Drug Dependence). In 2001, nearly sixteen million U.S. citizens aged 12 and older used an illicit drug in the previous month (Office of Applied Studies, Substance Abuse and Mental Health Statistics).

6. The proportion of eighth-graders using an illicit drug in the past year doubled from 1991–1995 (11 percent to 21 percent). Almost 40 percent of high-school seniors reported use of some illicit drug in the previous twelve months, up from 30 percent in 1991. Overall, 50 percent of all adolescents have tried an illicit drug before graduation from high school.

7. The average age of the first use of any illicit drug is 12–14 years, and some adolescents use multiple drugs. These substances are associated with nearly 50 percent of fatal motor-vehicle accidents and homicides, and a significant proportion of adolescent suicides (Fishman 394).

8. Illicit drug use has declined among college students, but has increased among eighth- and tenth-graders: 32 percent of all eighth-graders, 39 percent of all tenth-graders, and 47 percent of all twelfth-graders report that they have tried illicit drugs.

9. Marijuana is widely used. More than 40 percent of 1995 seniors reported using marijuana at some point in their lives, 35 percent reported its use in the last year, 21 percent in the past month, and 5 percent report daily use (Fishman 394).

10. Cocaine use may be as high as 15–20 percent among all students (Shannon 337), which might itself be an underestimate of overall prevalence in the community because high-school dropouts are not considered in surveys of high school students, and dropouts have higher rates of substance abuse.

11. Overall, in the United States, thirty million people have tried cocaine; of these, 20 percent have become regular users, and 5 percent have developed a compulsive pattern of use.

There has been a dramatic increase in emergency room visits for cocaine use (Wooton 89). An assessment of urine screens for cocaine among infants and children visiting emergency rooms found that 5 percent tested positive for cocaine, and another 1–2 percent tested positive for alcohol or another drug (Shannon 337).

12. There were over 19,000 deaths from drug-induced causes in 1999 (National Center for Health Statistics).

13. In 2001, there were nearly fifteen million persons aged 18 or older with a serious mental illness (Office of Applied Studies, Substance Abuse and Mental Health Statistics). Nearly nineteen million U.S. adults, or nearly 10 percent of the U.S. population aged 18 or older, have some degree of a depressive disorder in a given year (National Institute of Mental Health).

14. At least 10–20 percent of adults have an episode of major depression at least once in their lifetimes; 10–15 percent of new mothers have a serious episode of depression in the first year of their children's lives, and 50 percent of mothers of children younger than five years are depressed (Krugman 23–24). Many of these individuals turn to alcohol and other substances of abuse to relieve their sorrow.

violently. PCP can cause one to feel good, but can also cause one to act violently. LSD can permit one to have wonderful experiences, but flashbacks are potentially debilitating.

Over time, tolerance develops to most drugs, meaning that one has to take more of the drug to get the same effect. As the desired effect is craved, a person spends time thinking about the next fix or hit of drug; addiction has developed. With addiction, a person's life revolves around the drug—its procurement and its effects. Denied of their drug, even mild-mannered persons can turn violent or turn to crime to get the money necessary for the next dose of drug.

Depending on the drug, overdoses may cause slurred or pressured speech, nervousness, irrational behavior (paranoid or delusional ideas), seizures, cardiac arrhythmias, respiratory depression, coma, and death.

Substance abuse in childhood, adolescence, and during pregnancy is especially dangerous because of the known and potential effects on the growing person. Some of these effects are physical, such as the fetal alcohol syndrome in an infant born to a woman who abused alcohol during pregnancy. Some of these effects are mental or emotional, such as too many bad trips (or flashbacks) with LSD, and the consequent intellectual and emotional damage suffered. Many young children become addicted because they are around parents using drugs and want to try them themselves. Others get involved in the drug trade because they want extra money; once involved, they then sample the drugs themselves.

Children who are the children of addicted persons may not be cared for adequately. They may be dirty, hungry, and unsupervised in their daily activities, including schoolwork. In spite of this, they may be the ones who really care for the addicted adults and handle family affairs. They make excuses for parents who must repeatedly miss work because of hangovers or overdoses. Frequently, they grow into adults who abuse substances themselves or who marry persons exactly like their addicted parents.

Persons who are depressed might appear sad, hostile, or have wildly fluctuating moods; they might engage in risk-taking behaviors. They might have slowed speech or mannerisms and might appear unkempt. Alternatively, some depressed persons hide their condition until its later stages.

Emotional Challenges

For the persons addicted, denial that a problem exists is initially operant; they can stop drinking, smoking, or using drugs whenever they want to do so. When it becomes clear that they cannot, denial still continues as they blame their use of substances on their circumstances or on their relatives. Covering up their absences at work or at important engagements occurs through lying themselves or enlisting family members to lie for them.

Depending on the drug abused, psychological effects vary. Some addicts show no overt signs. Others may show nervousness or inattention. Others may show apathy or irritability. Still others may demonstrate tendencies to violence, delusional thinking, or paranoid ideation. Certainly, the person's behaviors before addiction and after it are markedly different. There is a loss of dependability. Bills may not be paid. Commitments may not be honored.

The children of such addicted parents may feel shame and embarrassment. They may not want to invite friends over to visit because they are embarrassed about the state of their homes or their parents' conditions. They may feel guilty because they believe (or have been made to believe) that they have done something to cause the parent's addiction. They may also be the "head" of the household, running errands and caring for younger siblings. They may feel hopeless that the situation will never change and may fantasize about running away. Some actually do.

When children and adolescents are addicted to substances, they can encounter the same psychological effects of the addicting substance as do adults, but they are even more concerned about nondisclosure. They lie to cover their habit and will attempt to procure money for their habit by stealing or illegal activities. School performance may drop; in a few students, however, school performance may be maintained to "cover up" the addiction even more effectively.

As was mentioned earlier, persons with depression might appear sad and weepy or might appear hostile and belligerent. They might have difficulty sleeping or, alternatively, sleep too much. Similarly, they might eat too little or too much. They might prefer to be alone ("the loner").

Spiritual Challenges

Those affected by the addicted person may ask, "Why me?" They may wonder why God doesn't curtail the freedom of the addicted person so that the family can be saved. They may accuse God of heartlessness as the family falls apart. They may pray initially, but when prayers are not answered, they may abandon praying. They may want to find solace in a worshiping community, but when God has not answered their prayers or when the threat of disclosure becomes too great with continued attendance at church, they stop attending, especially if they perceive that people are talking about them or their families. They may refuse the efforts of the pastor to talk with them or to visit them at home.

For those addicted, they may pray that God remove their addiction, but their lack of will power and their attraction to the addiction prevents God from assisting in their recovery. They may lose their faith in God, although some persons draw closer to God even during their times of greatest addiction. As the addicted person prefers the substance to God, prayer life ceases. Such people may think that their sins are so great that there is no hope or forgiveness for them. Spiritual despair is a real possibility.

Spiritual despair is a genuine possibility when persons are depressed. Why does God let them be so unhappy? Why doesn't God relieve their pain and lighten their mood? Some depressed persons might ruminate on past wrongs—real or imagined. Many depressed persons have difficulty believing in a good, loving God who has their interests at heart.

Individual Responses

Individual responses to addictions can be to encourage those who are known or suspected to be addicted to seek help before they destroy themselves and their families. Knowing some resources in one's community (and even volunteering at a drug-abuse hotline) can also be an aid, either to an addicted person or to affected family members. It is best not to accuse the addicted person, for he may still be in a denial phase and accusations will only anger him, leading to more intense denial.

Individuals can be educated about the signs of substance abuse and when to be suspicious, especially in the case of children and adolescents who require prompt intervention to assure the most successful outcome so that they may live healthy, productive lives. Although the list of signs is too long to be included here, the more common signs are pressured speech; irrational behavior, speech, or ideas; hair-trigger mood changes, especially for the worse; tremulousness ("the shakes"); pupillary constriction or dilatation; and nasal sniffing. Remembering that persons who are depressed are at risk for substance abuse, one can be alert to the signs of depression (sadness, weepiness, hopelessness, new onset acting-out behaviors) and attempt to provide the depressed person with some assistance in terms of community resources. At other times, a mildly depressed person may need only a shoulder to cry on for a period of time until the depression lifts. Prayer is essential.

Congregational Responses

The congregation can bring in a speaker for the children and adolescents about the various types of substance abuse, signs of addiction, effects on the body and mind, and treatment options so that young people can be aware of the facts. It is good for parents and teachers to attend these sessions as well so that they, too, can learn and reinforce the speaker's message. Sometimes, the best speaker is someone who was previously addicted, because he can tell a real story that kids can understand. If such a person is a member of the congregation and is willing to share his story to help the children, so much the better.

From the religious point of view, children and adolescents can be reminded that their bodies are a gift from God, and abusing drugs is not a way to show gratitude because such behavior will injure the body. This message should not be made just by the pastor but by all who work with children. But, beware! If an adult who abuses her own body by smoking or overeating delivers this message, children and adolescents may well point out that the speaker should follow her own advice.

Children and adolescents may also approach a pastor or a teacher if their own parents have an addiction. Such children are frightened not only because they are "telling" on the parent, but also because they are afraid that the parent may get sick and die if the addiction continues. The pastoral staff needs to have a plan ready if children from their own congregation bring this information to them. Perhaps a fellow member of the congregation could talk to such a parent; depending on the situation, perhaps the pastor is the better person to do so. In any event, such information from a child should not be ignored, because it is a child's cry for help and will teach him how responsive the faith community is to his concerns. The congregation should be aware of resources available for the children of addicted parents in their community so that they can refer their young people to others with whom they are able to discuss their problems and who will understand. Above all, the congregation needs to be aware that there may be a number of persons in their midst whose addictions are well hidden and hold those individuals in prayer also.

The same is true for those who are depressed in a congregation. Many depressed people put on a happy face for others, effectively hiding their pain. Other depressed persons clearly show their distress. Regardless of the circumstances leading to the depression, pastoral leadership must be alert to the signs of depression noted above and to the likelihood of depression in persons who have incurred a loss in their lives recently, although sometimes the losses are not so obvious. Knowing that the depressed person may turn to alcohol or other drugs to relieve suffering, the pastoral team must be aware of resources in the community for depressed persons and be prepared to recommend that such persons seek help. In the body of Christ, we are all profoundly interdependent, and none of us is without weaknesses or failings. Assisting one person in pain alleviates a measure of the pain in the entire body. Praying for those in pain and loneliness in some way relieves our own pain and loneliness.

REFERENCES

Belcher, H., and Shinitzky, H. "Substance Abuse in Children." *Archives of Pediatric and Adolescent Medicine* (1998), 152:952–60.

Fishman, M., Bruner, A., and Adger, H. "Substance Abuse among Children and Adolescents." *Pediatrics in Review* (1997), 18:394–403.

Jellinek, M., and Snyder, J. "Depression and Suicide in Children and Adolescents." *Pediatrics in Review* (1998), 19:255–64.

Krugman S., and Wissow, L. "Helping Children with Troubled Parents." *Pediatric Annals* (1998), 27:23–29.

Schwartz, R. "Adolescent Heroin Use." *Pediatrics* (1998), 102:1461–66.

Shannon, M., Lacouture, P., Roa, J., et al. "Cocaine Exposure among Children Seen at a Pediatric Hospital." *Pediatrics* (1989), 83:337–42.

Takahashi, A., and Franklin, J. "Alcohol Abuse." *Pediatrics in Review* (1996), 17:39–44.

Wooton, J., and Miller, S. "Cocaine: A Review." *Pediatrics in Review* (1994), 15:89–92.

STATISTICS

Alcohol and Drug Use—Federal Sources

www.niaaa.nih.gov/databases/abdep2.txt
www.cdc.gov/nchs/fastats/alcohol.htm
www.ncadd.org/facts/numberoneprob.html
www.cdc.gov/nchs/fastats/druguse.htm
www.samhsa.gov/oas/oasftp.htm

Depression—National Institute of Mental Health

www.nimh.nih.gov/publicat/numbers.cfm

FOR MORE INFORMATION

Check local telephone listings under "alcoholism," "substance abuse," "treatment facilities," "drug testing," "mental health services" (might be under government listing), "addiction treatment/services," "counseling," and "self-help/support groups."

National Toll-Free Numbers

NAMI	1-800-950-6264
National Drug & Alcohol Referral Service	1-800-662-4357
Narcotics Anonymous	1-800-317-3222
National Clearinghouse for Alcohol & Drug Information	1-800-729-6686

LOCAL RESOURCES

_____

_____

_____

_____

_____

Chapter 13

Child Abuse

*F*our-year-old Sarah was frightened. Every night her father came into her room to put her to sleep. But what her father did hurt her and made her cry. She couldn't tell her mother because her father had said, "If you tell Mommy about our special secret, she'll make me go away. You don't want Mommy to get mad and fight with me, do you?" Sarah loved her mother and her father and didn't want to make anyone fight. So she let her father hurt her and tried not to cry out loud.

Eight-year-old Anton heard his mother coming home. She seemed to be drunk again. Anton hated those nights when his mother was drunk, because those were the nights that she would beat him. It wasn't Anton's fault that his mother hated his father. And Anton thought that she hated him, too, because he looked just like his father. Anton pretended to be asleep until he felt his mother's fists against his sheet-covered face. In silence, he cried.

〜〜〜〜〜〜〜

Physical Challenges

A physically abused child may have a number of physical injuries, depending on the type of abuse inflicted. Welts, bruises, and lacerations are common, some of which are in the shape of the object of injury (e.g., hand, belt loop, etc.). These kinds of markings, especially on body areas not usually subject to the usual injuries that children receive (e.g., the inner thighs), should raise the possibility that a child is being abused. Children with injuries about the face without a convincing story of how the injury occurred raise the same possibility. Young infants can also have mouth trauma with bleeding inflicted by an adult thrusting a bottle into the child's mouth to keep her quiet.

General Comments and Facts to Consider

An abused child is defined as one under eighteen years of age whose parent or other person legally responsible for his care inflicts, or allows to be inflicted, physical injury, sexual assault, or emotional trauma. A neglected child is a child under eighteen years of age whose physical, mental, or emotional condition has been impaired because of the failure to supply her with food, clothing, shelter, education, medical care, proper supervision or guardianship—or is a child who has been abandoned.

1. In 2000, three million referrals for child abuse were made across the United States (National Clearinghouse on Child Abuse and Neglect); not all of these children were *proven* to be abused. Because not all abuse is reported, approximately 1–2 million U.S. children (or 3–5 percent of the population younger than eighteen years) are believed to be physically abused, sexually molested, emotionally battered, or severely neglected each year (Krugman 23–24).

2. Child abuse is assumed to be the greatest cause of death for infants between six and twelve months of age; between one and six months of age, abuse is second only to SIDS as a cause of death. Repeat abuse occurs in at least 20 percent of children (Kottmeier 343).

3. Twelve hundred children died of abuse or neglect in 2000 (National Clearinghouse on Child Abuse and Neglect).

4. Of substantiated child abuse in 2000, 63 percent were neglect; 19 percent physical abuse; 10 percent sexual abuse; and 8 percent psychological abuse (National Clearinghouse on Child Abuse and Neglect).

5. In the United States, it is estimated that nearly 350,000 children (including 25 percent of preadolescent and adolescent girls) are sexually abused each year; this amounts to 9 percent of all reported sexual abuse cases in this country. Over 80 percent of these victims are female. Among girls, whites and Hispanics become victims less often than do blacks. Younger children are more likely than older children to be victims of chronic and repetitive abuse by someone known to them.

6. Of rape victims younger than eighteen years of age, 10 percent are under ten years old, and 25 percent are between the ages of ten and fourteen years. The median age of victims of molestation is eleven years, although molestation most commonly occurs at 4–8 years of age. Incest occurs primarily between the ages of 10–14 years (Sanfilippo 621).

7. Perhaps as many as 25 percent of women have a history of serious sexual abuse before eighteen years of age (Leventhal 769).

Other injuries are much more serious. Abused children can sustain broken bones, burns, head trauma, and blunt abdominal trauma to internal organs such as the liver and spleen. Broken arms or legs may be caused by an adult roughly pulling, or twisting a child's arm or leg. Burns can be inflicted through roughly extinguishing a lighted cigarette against a child's skin in an attempt to punish him. A more serious burn is inflicted when a parent immerses a child in scalding water to punish her for crying, wetting his underwear, or otherwise "misbehaving." Head trauma is usually inflicted by a blow to the head with a blunt object or by being thrown against a wall. Abdominal trauma is inflicted by punching or kicking the abdomen.

Sexual abuse may or may not leave overt signs. Forcing a child to witness sexually explicit material either in person or through the media is sexual abuse, but leaves no visible marks. Certainly, voyeurism, fondling, forcing a child to touch an adult's genitals, or oral contact with a child's genitals or insertion of a finger into the vagina or anus usually leaves no telltale marks. Forced or repeated penetration of the anus or vagina does leave marks. The vagina may be torn and bleeding after an acute, forced insertion. Chronically, over time, scarring occurs. Forced penetration of the anus may also cause tears and bleeding; over time, a child's anus is stretched and can gape open a bit, making stool leakage a problem. It should be kept in mind that both girls and boys can be forcibly and repeatedly sexually penetrated by an older person. Many adults tend to forget that young boys can be injured as well as young girls.

If a perpetrator has a sexually transmitted disease, a child may bear the signs of that infection as well. Such signs include a discharge from the vagina, penis, or anus; certain skin lesions or rashes in these areas; and painful urination or defecation.

Children who are neglected also bear physical signs. Frequently, they are dirty, unkempt, malodorous, malnourished, or dressed inappropriately.

Emotional Challenges

Children who have been abused are frightened. They fear a new round of abuse from the adults in their lives who have been abusing them. Hence, they monitor their behavior closely so as not to attract attention. They are also reluctant to disclose the abuse to others because they are afraid that they or the perpetrators will be punished. As incredible as it might seem, children tend to protect parents who abuse them. They, like all children, need parental love and support. Somehow, these children believe that the abuse is their fault, perhaps because the abusing parent has said it so often. Hence, they fear reprisals against themselves. They will lie to protect themselves and others against disclosure. Another reason that they fail to disclose is that they have a difficult time trusting any adult because of their experience with adults in their lives. If they disclose, will they be believed, or will they only receive more rejection—and possibly more abuse?

Fear leads to chronic anxiety. When will the abuser strike again? Depending on a child's temperament, this anxiety may be manifested in different ways. She may be quiet and shy, almost receding into the background, or she may act out in frustration and anger, which frequently merits her more abuse.

The self-esteem of abused children suffers when trusted adults abuse them. In a child's mind, he must not be worth much if a parent must beat or neglect him repeatedly. Children who are sexually abused feel that they, too, are worthless because they are being forced to do things that they do not want to do. In addition, they may feel soiled and dirty, especially if a male perpetrator ejaculates in or on them. If the perpetrator has a genital discharge or lesions, they feel even more soiled.

Verbal abuse frequently accompanies physical or sexual abuse. It is demeaning enough to be repeatedly beaten or sexually used, but to hear degrading comments intensifies the tragic effect. Belittling a child or making crude accusations against a child further lowers self-esteem. In abused children's minds, if their parents say they are no good, they must *really* be no good.

Because they cannot escape what is happening to them, abused children are sad and depressed. How long will the abuse go on? Is there no end? Unfortunately, for some children the end comes only through their running away or their suicide. Running away exposes them to the possibility of even greater abuse, especially violence and prostitution. In addition, they may have no food to eat, no place to stay, and no way to obtain health care, leading to a greater likelihood of poor physical health. Suicide is an enormous tragedy as the young person sees only one way out of his shame and pain.

> For perspective on the emotional lives of the perpetrators of child abuse, see chapter 14, "Violence."

Victims of child abuse who survive into their adulthood may be left with post-traumatic stress syndrome. Although this syndrome was first described in connection with soldiers returning from war, it is now understood to be applicable to anyone who has experienced a catastrophic event in his or her life. Flashbacks to the event(s) may occur, as well as long-term depression and feelings of worthlessness. In addition, chronic physical symptoms might be present such as fatigue, vague physical aches, and so forth.

Abused children who survive into adulthood may become abusers themselves, may have difficulty in establishing intimate relationships with other people, or may become violent criminals. Alternatively, they may be chronically depressed or experience mental illness. The sooner a child can be removed from an abusive situation and can receive professional help, the better the chance for her to make a recovery so that she can mature into a mentally healthy and competent adult.

Children who suffer from neglect may have many of the same feelings of low self-esteem as do children who are abused. After all, children believe that if they are neglected by the ones who are supposed to care the most for them, they must not be worth very much. Unless there are caring adults in such children's lives, verifying their self-worth, these children are likely to believe the tragic "mismessage" of worthlessness.

Spiritual Challenges

"I kept praying to God," said the little girl, "but he wouldn't make my daddy stop hurting me. Doesn't God love me anymore?" Children who are abused may lose their faith in a loving God who has their best interests at heart. In a child's mind, if God really loved her, wouldn't God try to stop her pain? Children can conclude that God doesn't exist, God doesn't love them, God doesn't care, or God is punishing them and is on the side of the abuser. All of those conclusions are tragically damaging to a child's spiritual life. For some children, it is enough to make them give up on God and the church entirely. "I tried to tell my teacher that the man was hurting me, but she wouldn't listen," said a boy who had been abused by a neighbor. "And she goes to church every Sunday, but she wouldn't believe me; she wouldn't help me. If that's all the good church is, I'm never going back."

The damage to a child's relationship with God can be even more marked if the abusing adult gives the child the impression, directly or indirectly, that God is on his side, and the child deserves the abuse as punishment. "If you tell on me, I'll be mad and God will be mad," said a parent to her abused and frightened child. "The Bible says I can hit you," says the parent who is beating a child with his fists. Actually, the Bible says that a child can be disciplined, but not in anger. Those who strike children with fists or objects are usually not only angry but also enraged. It is small wonder that children who hear such messages will reject God, perhaps for the rest of their lives. To be rejected by parents is difficult enough; to be rejected by God is to be a nothing. "I wish I had never been born; I wish God had never made me," was the mournful response of a child repeatedly abused physically, emotionally, and sexually over the course of four years.

Individual Responses

It is difficult for many adults to understand how other adults can physically or sexually abuse children. Hence, sympathy for abusing adults may be lacking. It must be remembered, however, that many abusive adults were themselves victims of abuse in their own childhood. Although that does not in any fashion excuse their behavior, it does help us to understand that behaviors learned in childhood can affect a person for the rest of his life, and, perhaps, the next generation as well. Both abused children and their abusing parents need prayers. Individuals may also feel the call to volunteer at a Child Abuse Hotline if one exists in their communities or to become foster parents for abused children.

Child abuse is a crime, and anyone knowing or suspecting such abuse is required to report it to the police or Child Protective Services (CPS) in their communities. It is important to remember that one is reporting the abused child and not the abuser, because unless one has direct evidence of who is actually the abuser, one is making assumptions that might be false. Private citizens are called to report illegal activities; they are not called to confront or investigate the perpetrators of them. The proper authorities have received special training to assess an abused child and his situation.

In speaking to a child whom you suspect might be abused, it is best not to lead her to say certain things. If the subject is brought up, open-ended questions are the best. For example, it is better to say, "How did you get the bruise on your face, Jimmy?" rather than say, "Your mother hit you again with her belt, didn't she?" In the first instance, the child can answer as he sees fit. In the second, he may be forced to lie (to protect the parent), or he may not know how to answer the question (e.g., mother hit him, but not with a belt, or father hit him with a belt). Keep in mind that a child is less likely to be forthcoming about the incident if the questioning adult is not known well by him or is not an authority figure (such as a police officer, teacher, pastor, etc.).

Congregational Responses

Pastors can preach about child abuse, highlighting Jesus' highly complimentary words about children. Although some congregants might cite verses from the Hebrew Scripture (most notably the book of Proverbs) that declare that the father who loves his child spares not the rod, evidence from the same book(s) can be cited to emphasize that such discipline is never to be administered in anger or with force "or they may lose heart" (Col. 3:21). Most episodes of child abuse, starting out as "discipline," are in fact administered by not only angry parents but enraged ones. Their superior size compared with a child's size places the child at an enormous disadvantage. There is no scriptural basis for condoning the abuse of children—physical, emotional, or sexual. In fact, Jesus' own comments that it would be better for a millstone to be tied about the neck of the one who causes a little one to be lost is both blunt and clear. Jesus also reminded adults that unless they became more like children they would not enter the kingdom of heaven. These words should not be dismissed with, "Jesus didn't really mean that." It seems wiser to take Jesus' comments at face value rather than to impute a meaning to them to satisfy one's own need to be right.

The pastoral staff should have a plan of action if one of the children from their congregation reports that she is being abused by a parent, relative, or neighbor. What should they do? Whom should they contact? Similarly, how will the staff react if the allegation of abuse is aimed at one of their own teachers or adult leaders? It is far better for the staff to be proactive rather than reactive when word of suspected abuse reaches them. Anger aimed at the abuser is a natural human reaction, but it must not get in the way of getting the proper assistance for the child. His needs and welfare take precedence.

Children and those who have abused them require professional help to work through the traumas and to become rehabilitated. Congregations should be aware of services in their own communities. In addition, a congregation should stand ready to assist one of its own families if one of the parents is incarcerated for child abuse. How can the members of the congregation assist a family in the midst of one of the worst trials it will ever face? What can they do for *this* family to promote the process of God's healing? Prayers for all children who are abused or neglected in any way *and* for those who abuse or neglect them should be a routine part of congregational prayer. This marks a community clearly as followers of Jesus, willing to pray not only for the victims but also for those who "trespass against us."

REFERENCES

Bloch, H. "Abandonment, Infanticide, and Filicide." *American Journal of Diseases of Children* (1988), 142:1058–60.

Dubowiz, H. "Prevention of Child Maltreatment: What Is Known." *Pediatrics* (1989), 83:570–77.

Garbarino, J. "The Psychologically Battered Child." *Pediatric Annals* (1989), 18:502–4.

Garbarino, J., and Sherman, D. "High-Risk Neighborhoods and High-Risk Families: The Ecology of Human Maltreatment." *Child Development* (1980), 51:188–98.

Kottmeier, P. "The Battered Child." *Pediatric Annals* (1987), 16:343–51.

Krugman, S., and Wissow, L. "Helping Children with Troubled Parents." *Pediatric Annals* (1998), 27:23–29.

Leventhal, J. "Have There Been Changes in the Epidemiology of Sexual Abuse of Children During the 20th Century?" *Pediatrics* (1988), 82:766–73.

Paradise, J., Rose, L., Sleeper, L., et al. "Behavior, Family Function, School Performance, and Predictors of Persistent Disturbance in Sexually Abused Children." *Pediatrics* (1994), 93:452–59.

Sanfilippo, J., and Schikler, K. "Identifying the Sexually Molested Preadolescent Girl." *Pediatric Annals* (1986), 15:621–24.

STATISTICS

www.calib.com/nccanch/pubs/factsheets/canstats.cfm
www.prevent-abuse-now.com/stats.htm

FOR MORE INFORMATION

Check local telephone listings under "child welfare," "protective services" (under government listings), "child abuse," "support groups," and "family services."

National Toll-Free Numbers

Family Stress Hotline	1-800-243-7337
Child Management Services	1-800-422-4453

LOCAL RESOURCES

_____

_____

_____

_____

_____

Chapter 14

Violence

*T*welve-year-old Jeffrey is sitting in the hospital emergency room. He is angry, scared, and in pain. Several older boys had just jumped him in order to get his jacket. When he resisted, they stabbed him in the face, arms, and legs. How he wishes his dad would arrive! His father would take care of those guys for him.

Rachel was raped three weeks ago and has still not returned to work. She is too afraid that her assailant, who has not yet been apprehended, will find her. Rachel just sits at home and cries, cursing her stupidity for stopping at the convenience store after 10:00 P.M. Her mother repeatedly asks her, "Where was your mind? Everyone knows that sensible people don't go out after dark!" Such comments make Rachel feel worse.

Vicki is spending the night at a shelter for battered women. She had tried to leave her husband before, after he had broken her ribs in a fight, but he was so sorry that she went back to him. But after last night, when he tried to set her bed on fire after she had burned dinner, she knew she had to leave. "Why do I make him so angry?" she asks herself. "He's such a nice guy when he's not mad."

Physical Challenges

Victims of violence, like victims of child abuse, may be left with a variety of injuries depending on the weapon used. Bruises, lacerations, burns, gunshot wounds, blunt head or abdominal trauma all can leave the victim with varying degrees of acute injury and chronic physical impairment. Some victims

Facts to Consider

1. There are over 16,000 homicides in this country each year, more than any industrialized country in the world. Homicide is the twelfth leading cause of death in the United States and the leading cause of death for black youth 15–34 years of age (National Center for Health Statistics).

2. In 2000, there were over 1.4 million incidents of violent crime to people over age 12 in the United States per year (FBI Uniform Crime Rates); 33 percent of these victims sustain an injury, and these injuries cost three-quarters of a billion dollars per year.

3. There are four million reported cases of domestic abuse each year; one can only guess about the number of those never reported. More than ten million children per year witness a physical assault between their parents (Augustyn 35–37). Over 90 percent of domestic violence victims are female; every nine seconds, a U.S. woman is battered (American Institute on Domestic Violence).

4. Family violence accounts for 21,000 hospitalizations, nearly 100,000 hospital days, 28,700 emergency room visits, and 39,000 doctor visits per year, all costing over $44 million per year (Rivara 421). Between one and two thousand children die each year as a result of child abuse and neglect (Finkelhor 418).

5. A study from the Midwest revealed that childhood victims of abuse or neglect were more likely than nonabused/nonneglected individuals to have a juvenile or adult arrest. Almost 50 percent of victims of childhood abuse and neglect had been arrested by age 32 for a nontraffic offense (Maxfield 390).

6. From 1989 to 1994, the arrest rate for serious violent crimes (murder, rape, robbery, and aggravated assault) rose 46 percent. From 1985 to 1994, the rate of homicides committed by youth 14–17 years of age increased by 172 percent, whereas homicides committed by those older than age 25 in the same time span have been decreasing (Song 531–32).

7. Young people are not only the perpetrators of violent crimes, they are also the most frequent victims of crimes committed by youth. Youth aged 16–19 years have the highest risk for victimization by violent crime and are the group at greatest risk for nonfatal violence (Rivara 421).

8. Compared with individuals older than nineteen years, 12–19-year-olds experience three times as many rapes, two times as many robberies, and three times as many assaults. A recent random national telephone survey of two thousand 10–16-year-olds found that 41 percent had been victimized in some fashion. Of 3,700 high-school students, 33–44 percent of male students reported being struck at school within the past year, with 75 percent of males and females from large city schools reporting having witnessed someone being beaten up in school in the previous year. Moreover, 47 percent of first and second-graders had witnessed a shooting, and 31 percent had witnessed a stabbing (Song 531–32).

9. Twenty-five percent of 10–16-year-olds (or 6.2 million youth, based on a U.S. Census Bureau population of twenty-four million) have witnessed or have been a victim of violence; 327,000 experience some form of assault or abuse every year. One out of eight (or 2.8 million) experience an injury, and one out of a hundred (250,000) youth need medical care as a result of these injuries. In addition, over two thousand children aged 0–17 years are victims of homicide (Finklehor 418). Unimaginably, in 1993, fifty-seven children under fifteen years of age were murdered in Chicago (Ristow 16).

10. African American children and young adults are 3–10 times more likely than white counterparts to be homicide victims. Between 1987 and 1991, in west Philadelphia, there was a 179 percent increase in the number of firearm-related events affecting primarily the African Ameri-

can population. In Chicago, between 1986 and 1992, the incidence of gun assaults increased by 155 percent among children younger than age 16. Of 1,035 south-side Chicago students, aged 10–19 years, 40 percent had witnessed a shooting, 35 percent a stabbing, and 25 percent a murder. Prolonged exposure to violence may lead to psychological effects. In this study, of 146 children aged 7–13, 42 percent had seen someone shot, 37 percent had seen someone stabbed, 21 percent lived with someone who had been shot and 16 percent with someone who had been stabbed. Moreover, 47 percent of the girls and 55 percent of the boys had witnessed violence, and 43 percent of the children worried about getting hurt at school (Sheehan 502).

11. Nearly every major city tells the same story. A study of two Philadelphia middle schools (one urban and one suburban) revealed that:

- 96 percent and 89 percent of the students in the two schools, respectively, knew someone who had been robbed, beaten, stabbed, shot, or murdered.
- 88 percent and 59 percent, respectively, had witnessed a robbing, beating, stabbing, shooting, or murder.
- 67 percent and 40 percent, respectively, had been personally robbed, beaten up, stabbed, shot, or caught in gun cross fire.
- 73 percent and 59 percent, respectively, reported hearing gunfire in their neighborhoods.
- 97 percent and 82 percent, respectively, knew a victim, witnessed an event, or was a victim.

Most students had psychological symptoms following the episode (Campbell 396).

12. Twenty percent of Baltimore children (mean age twelve years, 96 percent African American) reported that they had been victims of violence or had been asked to sell illegal drugs. Ten percent had been raped or threatened with rape, shot, or knifed. Children exposed to violence have behavior problems/distress symptoms (Li 572) and are at risk to grow into violent adults.

13. In Washington, D.C., 45 percent of first- and second-graders had witnessed a mugging, 47 percent a shooting, 31 percent a stabbing, and 39 percent a dead body. Ten percent of children attending Boston City Hospital's Primary Care Clinic had witnessed a shooting or stabbing before age 6, half of them in their own homes and the other half in the streets near their homes. Ninety percent of New Orleans fifth-graders had witnessed a violent event, and 40 percent had seen a dead body. In Los Angeles, it is estimated that a child is present for 50 percent of rapes occurring at home, with 10 percent directly witnessing the rape (Augustyn 35–37).

14. In 1994, 13 percent of 12–13-year-olds and 17 percent of 14–17-year-olds reported carrying a weapon during the preceding twelve months (Augustyn 35–37).

15. Nine percent of students aged 12–19 years have been crime victims in or around their school in the previous six months; 25 percent of these students express fear of school. Twenty percent of high-school students carried weapons for self-protection in the month prior to being surveyed (Rivara 421). Ten percent of all children attending school are frightened through most of the school day (Garrity 90).

16. Intention to use violence in hypothetical situations is positively correlated with increasing age, lower church attendance, frequency of smoking, alcohol use, cocaine use, marijuana use, smokeless tobacco use, injecting drug use, depression, and exposure to violence. Adolescents who attended church regularly were less likely to report that they would use violence to resolve interpersonal conflict (DuRant 1104).

of violence become chronically disabled because of their injuries. For most victims of violence, the acute physical injuries pale in contrast to the emotional injuries with which they are left.

Emotional Challenges

The emotional challenges that a victim faces depend, in part, on whether the act was random by a stranger or intentional by a known party.

For persons who have sustained an injury due to a random act of violence, they may be afraid to venture out of their houses again, afraid that every stranger is a potential assailant. They may fear persons who remotely remind them of their assailant. They may be afraid to go anywhere alone. If the attack was very serious, such as rape or aggravated assault with a knife or gun—even without a lethal weapon—a person may be consumed with fears that it could happen again or that the assailant could return. Because such persons have been demeaned, their self-esteem suffers. Especially in the acute aftermath of an attack, they may not be able to function in their daily activities; their ability to concentrate is limited.

Some victims repeatedly replay the mental tape of the entire event, castigating themselves with guilt for not doing something differently. "Why did I go to the mall that night?" "Why didn't I lock my car door?" "Why didn't I take my usual way home?" Such replaying simply serves to heighten their own guilt that the crime was their fault, and that if they had been smarter, it would not have happened. This further erodes self-esteem. Depending on the injuries sustained, a victim may be constantly reminded of the event, never able to shake it completely from his mind.

Victims of crime may be very tearful and depressed; alternatively, they may be very angry, acting out their hostilities with family members, friends, and coworkers. This latter method of handling the aftermath of violence is more common in males, whereas the former is more common in females. Alternatively, some victims act as if nothing significant happened, bottling up their emotions and reactions. The victim who is getting over her trauma too well or too rapidly may be in denial or may be internalizing more than anyone realizes.

Tension can rise at home but is not usually the fault of the other family members who are trying to be supportive. Many times, the victim is not sure what he needs, and so it is difficult for others to anticipate those needs. Performance at home, school, or work can suffer.

Children who have been victims of crime have many of the same reactions as do adults. They may cry or act out. Their eating, sleeping, and ability to play may be seriously compromised, especially shortly after the event. These reactions are also true of children whose parents have been victimized. Such children may be very fearful, afraid to permit the parents to leave the house. Frequently, they are afraid to go to school lest something happen to the parent in their absence. In their own minds, they take on the role of "protector" of the parents.

The victim (and his family) of a random crime wonders when, if ever, life will become normal again, and mourns the life he once had.

The victim of an intentional crime by a known party (such as spousal abuse) also lives in fear and sadness, and wonders if her life will ever be normal. Although victims of intentional crime may not fear strangers as do victims of random crimes, they fear encountering the abuser, especially in a secluded place. In addition, they have a more pervasive sense of having deserved the abuse. "What should I expect—I married a guy like my father, who always beat my mother," said a woman hiding in a shelter. Like an abused child, the victims of domestic violence may think the abuse is completely their fault: "If I didn't make him so mad by doing stupid things, he wouldn't have to hit me," the same woman remarked. Like an abused child, they will lie to protect themselves and the perpetrator. "Clumsy me—I walked into a door again last night in the dark," said a woman whose coworkers worried about the unusual bruises on her body. Like an abused child, she will protect and defend the abuser. One woman told her pastor, "He's a really good guy; he just has a temper, that's all. Doesn't everybody?"

Victims can suffer from post-traumatic stress disorder, experiencing a myriad of physical complaints, depression, and an inability to concentrate. They may also turn to alcohol or drugs in an attempt to escape the miserable lives they are forced to live.

Children who witness violence in their homes and in their neighborhoods are also left with emotional scars. *They* are also victims of violence. Some grow into adults lacking empathy for others, placing them at risk for violent behaviors as well. This hardening may occur as early as the first decade of life for both the victims and witnesses of violence. Although it is probably brought into play as a defense mechanism for a young child, it can all too easily become a permanent part of his personality, making the likelihood of development into an emotionally mature adult nearly nonexistent.

What can be said of the perpetrators of violence? Whether they are abusing a child, a known relative or friend, or a stranger, those who perpetrate violence have poor impulse control. When they want something, they want instant gratification. If they don't get what they want as soon as they want it, no matter how unreasonable that is, they lash out in violence. They are also immature, taking only their own wants into consideration and not the needs or wants of their victims.

Although some perpetrators of violence are completely antisocial (most notably those who prey on strangers), others function well in society, choosing only a single person (child, spouse, friend) upon whom to unleash their frustrations. When these individuals are accused of violence, neighbors might be very surprised about their shadow side: "But she was such a nice neighbor." "He was a model husband."

Some male abusers have problems only with females, especially those who resemble their mothers, sisters, ex-wives, and so forth; others have problems with all females. In the case of rape, the crime is less a sexual one than one of power, as the man uses his physical power to humiliate and incapacitate a woman, perhaps because he feels that he has been humiliated and incapacitated by women in his own life.

Many perpetrators of violence, including most inmates in prisons, have been victims of child abuse or sexual abuse themselves; lacking an adequate level of self-esteem, they deny one to others. In addition, many of these perpetrators are subject to addictions to alcohol or other drugs; in fact, their tendency to abuse may be heightened when they are high or when they are in desperate need of their next fix.

Individuals who abuse may be in complete denial of how sick they are, and, instead, point the finger of blame at their victims. "She knows that when she burns dinner, she's going to upset me." "It wasn't my fault I raped her—she was asking for it with the dress she had on."

Spiritual Challenges

"Where was God when I was being attacked?" asked the weeping victim of a rape. "Where is God when my husband keeps beating me?" asks another. "What have I done wrong to deserve this kind of treatment?" asks a man shot by a complete stranger.

Victims of random violence wonder where the God who sees all and knows all was when they were made victims. Victims of domestic violence wonder where the God of love is when they must endure daily abuse. Such persons may stop praying because "praying doesn't work," as one battered woman said sadly. They may stop attending church services because they do not want to endure the stares and questions of others. They may not be sure if there really is a God to worship.

Alternatively, they may be angry at God. "If God won't help me, I don't need him. Where was he when I really needed him?" asked the victim of a drive-by shooting. "If God won't clean up our neighborhood from the drug dealers, who needs him?" asked a bitter mother whose son was murdered by drug dealers shooting at each other. Some victims of violence may believe that God is on the side of the abuser and entirely against them. "My husband always said that Scripture says that men can do whatever they want with their wives, and wives can't do anything about it. Is that true?" asked a woman physically abused over the course of a ten-year marriage. Said another battered woman, "If God was on my side, why didn't he stop my husband?" The notion of a God on the side of the abuser may sadden them so profoundly that they enter into a spiritual depression. "I always learned that 'If God is for us, who can be against us?'" said one woman. "But I say if God is against you, what difference does it make who is for you? And, somehow, I feel that God is not for me anymore, and I don't know how to make it better."

Individual Responses

It is easy for us to try to ignore an act of random violence that has happened to an acquaintance. Perhaps the victim doesn't want to talk about it or continue to be reminded about the event. Perhaps talking about it reminds us how vulnerable we are, for we are just like the victim in so many ways. Perhaps our own fear makes us want to ignore that such a thing has even happened. In the case of domestic violence, we might be tempted to judge, saying things like, "Well, she knows he's a loser; she's asking for it if she stays with him" or "She deserves what she permits." Such attitudes do not do justice to the Christian imperative to love our neighbor as ourselves. If we were in such circumstances, would we really want others to judge us—or to listen to us and help us if they can?

Granted, many victims of domestic abuse, out of their great fear, do not want interference from outsiders. One should not, however, automatically assume that to be true for every battered woman. Many abused women have longed for *someone* to notice their recurrent black eyes or bruises and to make the first contact, but no one did. For some of these women, they feel less guilt in discussing their problems if they are not the first ones to raise them; it is safer if someone else does so.

Certainly, private citizens should not take the law into their own hands and try to "handle" the abuser, for the abuser may turn his violence on the person trying to be of assistance or take it out on the victim, thereby paving the way for the victim to endure even more abuse. Anonymous tips, however, can be given to police departments and to community-based domestic abuse hotlines. Persons interested in assisting women in crisis can volunteer at such a crisis hotline in their communities.

Both domestic abuse and random violence are crimes, and, as such, they should not be ignored because they are "none of my business." If we permit violence to exist in our homes, we encourage it in our streets. If we permit today's children to witness violence in their homes and in our streets, we will have yet another generation of persons who believe that violence is a realistic way to solve problems.

Congregational Responses

There are probably several abused women or children in every congregation. That is difficult for most congregants to hear because no one wants to believe that violence is so close to home. It is easier to believe that there are no abused women or children in one's congregation because they would "look different" somehow, making their presence obvious. This is not the case.

Because there are abused women in nearly every congregation, congregations must be proactive. What steps would they take if they discovered that one of their own women or children was being abused? What would they do as a congregation and as individuals in that congregation? At the very least, all citizens should know what the law requires in their jurisdiction and which emergency shelters, hotlines, or other services are available for both victims and potential perpetrators in their communities. For example, a number of communities have a hotline for parents who are potentially abusive so that the parent can "talk it out" rather than "take it out" on a child.

If there are a number of abused women in a congregation, the pastoral team might consider starting a support group for them. Similarly, if there have been several congregants who have been the victims of crime, a support group for them might be considered. It is important to stress that the right person must lead a support group. Because of the intense psychological issues that will surface, the leader must be someone who is trained in handling such issues. If a congregation does not have such a person, the pastoral team should investigate appropriate community resources and know how to access them for their congregants.

Pastors should preach on the entire issue of violence—both domestic and random. The pastor is in an excellent position to explain that certain biblical texts were never meant to sanction abuse by a husband toward his wife (or vice versa). Indeed, husbands are called to love their wives as Christ loves the church—hardly a destructive relationship! Similarly, wives are called to love their husbands as the church loves Christ.

When a member of the congregation has been the victim of random violence, the pastor can remind the congregants that they are called to become involved—just as the Samaritan became involved with the battered Jew (his "natural" enemy). Several people passed by the injured man but did not help him, each for his own reason. Jesus did not applaud their behavior or make excuses for them. Instead, he emphasized that true neighborliness was embodied in the Samaritan. We are called to do no less, for whatever we do to the least of our brothers and sisters, we do to Christ. Reaching out to an injured person may be as simple as a card or a telephone call. It may be offering to watch a child, doing the family's shopping, or carpooling the children to school. It certainly includes keeping the victims of violence in private and community prayer. However, one might be called to become more involved than those simple gestures. But the point is that we are all called to do something to relieve pain in another person's life. In other words, we are called to mirror Christ to a person in need.

And finally, a congregation should not become complacent regarding the reality of violence in our society just because the church is located in a "good" neighborhood. Violence can occur anywhere. In addition, complacency implies that it is "someone else's problem, not ours." This is an unconscionable stance for Christians who believe in the reality of the body of Christ, for when one member of the body suffers, we all suffer. When one member is diminished, we are all diminished. We all must live in the world, and other people's actions *do* affect our lives; other people's children *do* affect our children. When inadequate schools are permitted for certain students, when poverty is allowed to flourish in the midst of plenty, when racism is present but unopposed, when injustice screams for a response but is met with silence, we not only get what we deserve, we demonstrate our reluctance to hear (and maybe even our loathing of) Jesus' message, preached by his words, actions, and death.

REFERENCES

Augustyn, M., Parker, S., Groves, B., et al. "Silent Victims: Children Who Witness Violence." *Contemporary Pediatrics* (August 1995), 12:35–57.

Campbell, C., and Schwartz, D. "Prevalence and Impact of Exposure to Interpersonal Violence among Suburban and Urban Middle School Students." *Pediatrics* (1996), 98:396–402.

Duffy, S., McGrath, M., Becker, B., et al. "Mothers with Histories of Domestic Violence in a Pediatric Emergency Department." *Pediatrics* (1999), 103:1007–13.

DuRant, R., Treiber, Fr., Goodman, E., et al. "Intentions to Use Violence among Young Adolescents." *Pediatrics* (1996), 98:1104–8.

Finkelhor, D., and Dziuba-Leatherman, J. "Children as Victims of Violence: A National Survey." *Pediatrics* (1994), 94:413–20.

Garrity, C., and Baris, M. "Bullies and Victims." *Contemporary Pediatrics* (February 1996), 13:90–116.

Knapp, J., and Dowd, M. D. "Family Violence." *Pediatrics in Review* (1998), 19:316–21.

Li, X., Howard, D., Stanton, B., et al. "Distress Symptoms among Urban African American Children and Adolescents." *Archives of Pediatric and Adolescent Medicine* (1998), 152:569–77.

Maxfield, M., and Widom, C. "The Cycle of Violence." *Archives of Pediatric and Adolescent Medicine* (1996), 150:390–95.

Ristow, K. "Put Away Your Sword: Addressing the Issue of Violence in Our World. *Catechist* (March 1994), 16–18.

Rivara, F., and Farrington, D. "Prevention of Violence." *Archives of Pediatric and Adolescent Medicine* (1995), 149:421–29.

Sheehan, K., DiCara, J., LeBailly, S., et al. "Children's Exposure to Violence in an Urban Setting." *Archives of Pediatric and Adolescent Medicine* (1997), 151:502–4.

Song, L., Singer, M., and Anglin, T. "Violence Exposure and Emotional Trauma as Contributors to Adolescents' Violent Behaviors." *Archives of Pediatric and Adolescent Medicine* (1998), 152:531–36.

STATISTICS

www.cdc.gov/nchs/fastats/homicide.htm
www.disastercenter.com/crime/uscrime.htm
www.aidv-usa.com/Statistics.htm

FOR MORE INFORMATION

Check local telephone listings under "domestic violence," "women's services" (might be under government listings), "victim assistance," "rape," "crisis intervention," "domestic violence hotline," and "support groups."

National Toll-Free Numbers

Family Stress Hotline	1-800-243-7337
National Youth Crisis Hotline	1-800-448-4663

LOCAL RESOURCES

_____

_____

_____

_____

_____

Chapter 15

Media

Six-year-old Kevin is home from school. After lunch he sits with his mother on the sofa as she watches the "soaps." Kevin is confused about what he is seeing, but when he talks, his mother tells him to shut up. Yet he wonders why all those ladies and men are in bed with each other.

Sadie is an older woman living alone and on a fixed income. Her son rents videos and watches them with her. Last week, he rented a video about a serial killer. Although Sadie wouldn't watch it because it scared her, she could hear the screams of the victims. That really upset her. Now she is afraid to stay alone. Her son reminds her that it was only a video, but she can still hear the screams.

It is three weeks before Christmas, and Colleen is driving her parents crazy. Every toy that she sees advertised she wants. Her parents have tried to turn off the television set, but Colleen just screams. She's even worse when she is in a store. "She's so selfish and grabby," her mother complains.

∽∽∽∽∽∽∽

Physical Challenges

Except in the cases of copycat crimes or the making of explosives, exposure to the media may not harm someone physically. There have been a number of victimizations of individuals by adults (and even children) by those who were copying something that they had seen on television, in a video, or in a movie. In addition, children and adults attempting to make explosives from information available on the Internet have sometimes had the results literally blow up in their faces, injuring not only themselves but others and their property.

116

Children who watch many hours of television or who sit at a computer for hours on end, day after day, tend to be heavier, because they substitute a sedentary activity for more active ones. In addition, many children snack as they sit at the computer or watch television. This snacking is prompted by the type of food ads on television that children are likely to see: high-calorie, low-nutrition, sugary, or fried "junk" foods. The consequences of childhood obesity and lack of physical activity may last for decades and may even shorten one's life.

Emotional Challenges

The media may make many individuals feel very deprived; after all, who can really afford the latest fashions, toys, cars, appliances, and the like without going into debt? Because the media make it seem that everyone can have all the goodies they want, those who can't feel woefully inadequate and resentful of those who can have it all. Alternatively, people go into debt to create the impression that they, too, can have it all.

Another sense of inadequacy is in the realm of sexual behavior. Again, who can really have *any* person of one's choice? Who really has the body of a model—except a model? Yet, by seeing these images constantly the viewer is reminded of what a loser she really is, and will always be.

This sense of being a loser extends to the very idea of family. Families on television are attractive and likeable; how many of our own families are consistently that pretty, funny, and that well behaved? Children, especially those from broken homes, feel more deprived than ever by watching families on most prime-time television programs. Siblings always resolve differences by the end of the program (usually thirty minutes), and parents are always kindly, never out of control. How does this compare with real-life families?

Fear can also be a response to watching a great deal of television or particular movies or videos. The world is a dangerous place; even one's neighbors might be bad people and try to hurt one or one's family. Hence persons overstate their risk of victimization and curtail their daily activities in response to the media's portrayal of life in their city or neighborhood.

Certain types of media don't just make children more violent, they make the rest of us more aggressive, too. After watching a "shoot 'em up" movie or a video about a town terrorized by a maniac killer, many persons feel like taking the law into their own hands. Unfortunately, some of the more unstable do just that.

Entitlement abounds on television: "You're number one; you deserve it." One can do whatever it takes to get what one deserves—even being rude to

General Comments and Facts to Consider

Media are so pervasive in our culture. It seems that we can't go anywhere without hearing a radio or television set blasting in our ears. Even stores have televisions that patrons can view while they are waiting for the next salesperson or are in the checkout line.

Media in and of themselves are not evil; it all depends on the message that the media send. When media send wholesome messages, media act responsibly. There are many wholesome television programs, videos, movies, and magazines. In addition, there are many fine educational programs and publications, and these deserve to be used. However, when any of the media send hurtful or inappropriate ones, by reasonable people's standards, media act irresponsibly.

In this chapter, the term *media* includes radio, television (standard and cable), videos, Internet, books, newspapers, and magazines.

1. According to Nielsen data, the average American child views 21–23 hours of television per week. By the time today's children reach seventy years of age, they will have spent 7–10 years of their lives watching television. Because 98 percent of all American homes have a television set, television is the single most important medium in the lives of children. Although movies and videos are likely to be more violent than television, there is still much violence presented on television. The level of prime-time violence is 3–5 violent acts per hour, and during Saturday morning programming, there are 20–25 violent acts per hour. Over one thousand studies attest to a causal relationship between media violence and aggressive behavior in some children. Because prior to the age of eight years children cannot always discriminate between real-life and fictional violence, the effects of viewing television violence are more marked at younger ages. The fear is that children might learn that violence is an acceptable way to solve problems (AAP Statement on Media Education).

This is true not only for young children but also for adolescents and adults who may believe that the world is as violent as their favorite television program. This mentality may be reinforced by the evening news in which the viewer sees bloodstains of the victim on the sidewalk or chalk marks where the dead victim was found, or the victims of crime and their distraught relatives who look just like the viewer.

2. In the various forms of media, sexual exploitation is also common, and sexual morality is nonexistent; the media frequently glorify stars who are sexually immoral. In movies, videos, and television programs, unmarried people sleep with each other with great regularity. Rarely are the consequences of unprotected sex—such as unwanted pregnancies, sexually transmitted diseases, physical and emotional pain—ever adequately portrayed. Women wear very revealing clothing on television and in magazines, especially those directed to male readership. Males are not "real" men unless they conquer each women whom they desire. Magazine covers scream with such titillating headlines as "Super Sex—Every Time!" "Make Your Man Scream for Joy!" "Orgasms You'll Never Forget!"

3. The commercialism of television is also an issue of deep concern. Americans are among the most materialistic in the world—at the expense of many poorer countries. A materialistic mentality insists that one must always have what is new (or improved), no matter what the cost. Nowhere is there any injunction against throwing perfectly usable (but out-of-date) items away. The push by the media to "buy, buy, buy" is aimed at children as well as adults. Otherwise, why is there such a burst of toy commercials after Thanksgiving in this country? Why are there so many ads for candy around Easter or Valentine's Day? The media want consumers to

believe that they are losing out unless they have the latest toy, the best chocolate, or the newest fashions. High-volume ads blare out from radio stations and from television programs. Full-page color ads take over page after page of popular magazines and newspapers. Young children implore their parents for sweets in the supermarkets and for toys in toy stores. Adolescents beg their parents for money so they can go to the mall to get new clothes, records, or magazines. Adults go on a shopping spree when they feel down, buying things they don't really need or even want. Indeed, most citizens have been so successfully converted to a consumer way of life that they do not give alternative ways of living much of a second thought.

4. An increasing danger of the electronic media (especially the Internet) is their easy access by children and mentally unstable persons who can easily find information that might prove dangerous to them, such as how to make explosives. Persons with an interest in child pornography can use the Internet to lure children. In the name of freedom of speech, anything goes—and has gone. In the name of freedom of speech, our children and mentally incapacitated persons may be exposed to victimization or issues beyond their understanding.

5. Records and CDs may glorify violence, racism, sexual exploitation (and even rape), profanity, and worship of the devil. Adolescents listen to and buy many hours of this music, which may be also visually depicted on MTV. For some unstable youngsters, listening to such music may lead them to repeat what they see or lead them to Satan worship.

others. And why not? Other people are only obstacles in one's way; they are only here to use as a stepping-stone toward achieving one's goals. Thus the media encourage a self-satisfied selfishness and a disregard for those who can't "cut it" or "get their act together."

Spiritual Challenges

Where is God in our media? God is nowhere to be found for the most part. Certainly God could not be portrayed side by side with rampant consumerism—not while a good part of the world lacks the basics of life, such as shelter, food, clothing. Certainly God cannot be portrayed side by side with overt violence and racism—not the God of love who made all people as God's own, and who weeps over the slaughter of innocents and the victimization of God's children across the globe. Surely God cannot be portrayed side by side with overt sexual immorality—not the God who abhors adultery, the God who decreed that both man and woman are good, and that they are to cling to each other as one flesh.

God has been given no significant place in our media, and that is what children learn. God's only place is on Sunday mornings with television evangelists or in the middle of the night when no one is watching anyway. In the case of certain television evangelists, they may lead more people away from God than to God because of their theatrics, which can lead to cynicism in a viewer whose faith is already precarious.

God is simply irrelevant to the media. The media do not encourage children or families—or anyone for that matter—to pray more. Instead, they urge us to buy more, have more sex, and to look out for number one. Sadly, number one is not God; it is our sad selves.

Individual Responses

The media are so prevalent; how can any of us hope to escape them? Yet on an individual level, there are a number of actions that can be taken to minimize the effect of the media. Each person might make more space in his or her life for quiet time each day, refusing to read, listen to, or watch the media during that time period. Such time helps one to be more centered, more intensely aware of life from one's own perspective rather than someone else's. If there are children in the household, they, too, can be encouraged to develop this time for quiet. Initially, children usually resist this, but eventually many children find this to be an opportune time to write in a diary, to sort things out, or to just admire nature.

Individual adults can also refuse to subscribe to as many magazines and newspapers as they may currently do. After all, we subscribe to these things because we feel we need to be on top of things, or that we will look foolish if we do not know as much as others. The truth of the matter is that we will never know as much as we would like to know, no matter how many books, newspapers, and magazines we read. Adoption of this step does not mean that we give up all reading material, but that we decide that two or three periodicals are essential to us, relinquishing the remainder.

The same holds true for television programs viewed, videos rented and watched, and radio programs heard. How much of these do we really need in our lives? Do we really need to cruise the television channels, watching the news from three different stations? Do we really need to see the latest videos as soon as they come out? It is also good to reflect on the kinds of programs we prefer. Are they ones promoting violence, materialism, sexism, or racism? Even though we might not be overtly violent, sexist, or racist in our own lives, our preferences tell us a great deal about our inner longings.

If there are children in the house, either as residents or as visitors, even more attention needs to be paid to the amount and types of media exposure that they receive. Many households have a television always on, and children passively watch whatever is there. Such programs may be most inappropriate for children. Similarly, some households have any magazines that have come into the home lying about on countertops or coffee tables, readily available for any set of eyes. Adults must pay close attention to what is easily at hand, not only for their own children or grandchildren, but also for young visitors.

Parents or grandparents should know those whom their children or grand-children visit. If certain media are not permitted in one's own home, why should children have access to them in another home? Because none of us can control the values of our neighbors, it might be necessary for us to limit our children's visits to those neighbors whose values do not agree with ours. But we must first know who our neighbors are before we can ever hope to know their values.

Watching television, videos, or movies with children and adolescents can be educational for all concerned. It can be educational for adults because they can learn what their children prefer in the way of entertainment and just how violent or materialistic that preference is. They can learn why a child or ado-lescent prefers a certain program and what sense he makes of it. It can be equally educational for children and adolescents to watch with an adult, espe-cially if that adult provides commentary on worrisome images or commer-cials. A few examples suffice: "What do you think of that commercial? Do you really think potato chips dance? What do they want you to do?" or "Why do you think that the robber beat up the older woman? Was that fair? What do you think about people who want other people's things and beat them up to get them?" or (for cartoons) "Did you see that truck run over the cat? The cat jumped right back up! Do you think that would happen in real life if a truck ran over a cat, a squirrel, a dog, or a person? What would happen in real life?" This is called proactive viewing, and studies have demonstrated its beneficial effect on children's understanding of the unreality of many television pro-grams (or videos) and the marketing techniques present in commercials.

In the case of adolescents, adults in their lives should be aware of the type of music they prefer. Although adolescents should have an area of privacy, that space should be negotiated with the parent and not assumed. Adolescents whose recent behaviors are radically different from their previous way of behaving and who lock themselves in their rooms for long periods of time deserve parental input to assure that they are not getting themselves into more trouble than they understand. In extreme cases, such as an adolescent fasci-nated by Satan worship, violence, or the tools of destruction, professional help should be sought.

Congregational Responses

As a congregation, the local church can offer adult education on the pervasiveness of media in our lives, and what we can do to curtail this pervasiveness and to ameliorate its effects. Particularly important are talks with and for children and adolescents so that they can learn both from each other and knowledgeable adults. Most children and adolescents are amazed to learn how many commercials they see in a year or how many acts of violence they will view on television, movies, or videos by the time they graduate from high school. The question can be put to them, "Do you really want someone else determining how you think and what you see for so many years?" The children and adolescents themselves can come up with suggestions for how to limit their own media exposure.

The pastor of a congregation can also provide insight into the effects of certain forms of media, working this into sermons occasionally. Granted, there is only so much that can be commented upon in the course of a year of sermons. But, given the pervasiveness of media and their potentially deleterious effects in our society, surely this merits a pastoral comment, because the media's message is so frequently antithetical to the Christian message.

It is also important for local and global church leaders to take a stand for God. Letter-writing campaigns can occur against particularly harmful programs, either from a local church or from the denominational/diocesan office. If pastors and church leaders will not raise their voices in support of the Christian message in the midst of so many conflicting voices all vying for attention, how can they expect the larger church membership to do so? In this life, God chooses to have no voice except those of human beings. If we who are believers in a good and loving God do not speak up, who will?

REFERENCES

American Academy of Pediatrics (AAP) Policy Statement, Committee on Public Education, "Media Education." *Pediatrics* (1999), 104:341–44.

AAP Policy Statement, Committee on Communications, "Media Violence." *Pediatrics* (1995), 95:949–51.

Strasburger, V., and Donnerstein, E. "Children, Adolescents, and the Media." *Pediatrics* (1999), 103:129–40.

FOR MORE INFORMATION

Contact local broadcasters in your area; libraries may also be a good source of information.

LOCAL RESOURCES

_____

_____

_____

_____

_____

Conclusion

So many problems, so many suffering people! How can we ever hope to make a difference in our troubled world?

If we were to tackle problems alone, if we had to devise solutions for the many problems discussed in this book, our chances for success would be limited. But, as persons of faith we are not alone. We are followers of the One who called us friends and who reminded us that whatever we do in his name, we do for him. With the early disciples, we are called to work with him to witness that the reign of God is indeed present.

Do we act as if God's reign is among us? Could nonbelievers know by our words and, of more importance, by our actions that we believe in God? Do we act as if we are part of a very large family and that each man, woman, and child is a sister or brother in that family? Do we act as if we have confidence in God's sovereignty? Or do we act as if the powers of the world are too much for even God?

If we are to be faithful sons and daughters of God, then we are to live in hope and trust. By ourselves we can do nothing. But God is with us. God's grace enables us to move forward and to do what we can do in any given situation. But we must be willing to take a risk and let God's grace touch us in profound ways. We must allow God to have God's way with us. We must be willing to align our free will with God's will. Cooperating with God's grace might take us to places where we would not otherwise have gone. It might engage us in activities in which we would not otherwise have been engaged. Cooperating with God might be the most lofty thing we can ever do, but it frequently is not a safe thing to do, and it just might be risky.

But Christianity is not about safety on earth; it is about the risk of following Christ more closely with each and every day. When Jesus walked this earth, he was usually found in some of the poorest, saddest, and riskiest places on earth. It is no different for the living Christ today, and it should be no different for us.

Christ knew human nature very well, and so he told his disciples to count the cost of following him. We are given the same message. It was no more possible for Jesus' disciples to meet the needs of each person who came to them any more than it is possible for us to do so. There were—*and still are*—too many needy people to believe that a ministry is a "once and for all" project. Jesus warned his disciples that the poor would always be with them. So are the many problems that human beings have, either as a result of their own actions, those of others, or those for which no blame can be assigned.

If problems will always be with us, why try to solve them? If the problems will outlive us, why bother? If we'll never succeed in eradicating a problem or crossing it off a "to do" list, then why not resign ourselves to reality so that we will be less frustrated?

As Mother Teresa noted, we are not called to be successful, but to be faithful. Our ministry is not to problems but to people—one person at a time. As Christians, it is our reaching out to one person at a time.

That is important, for this is the evidence that God's reign is near. The world says it is foolhardy or impossible to try to solve problems on a global scale; there are just too many and there is not enough time or money, even if we wanted to do so. But the Christian sees the individual with the problem, not the problem of the individual. The Christian remains faithful by ministering to living individuals, not to problems per se. Even community advocacy work, directed toward solving some problem, is first and foremost about individuals—*people* who have a problem. And at any given time in our lives, *we* might be the one with the problem. We might need others' ministry *to us.*

We will need energy for the ministry ahead of us, for it is easy to become discouraged because our efforts will not always result in the outcomes that we want. Those to whom we are ministering might reject, refuse, or trick us, just as we might do the same to those who minister to us.

Because we are in ministry for the long haul, we need to follow Jesus' example and advice: pray, do not work alone, eat well, and take some time away for rest and renewal. This is true both for congregations and for individuals. For example, nowhere is it written that a congregation must solve a community problem itself. Yet how often is there evidence of congregations working with other congregations to solve a common problem? The more usual response is for one congregation to *define* itself by a particular ministry with an almost "hands-off" stance toward other congregations that might like to become involved. This is bad theology and bad ministry. It is not supported by Scripture.

Another temptation for a congregation (or an individual) is to think that it can do all things well, that it can have a plethora of ministries. Unfortunately, individuals fall into this way of thinking also. It is preferable to do a few things *really* well than many things only adequately, or even poorly.

We are *all* members of the body of Christ; we all affect and are affected by others. Their joys should be our joys; their sorrows, ours. When we are weak, they are called to be strong for us; when they are weakened, we are called to build them up. This is not some pie-in-the-sky mentality but is the very one that underlies the healthy functioning of the human body. All organs, all cells are there for the good of the whole. When there is a problem in the body, each organ is affected. Each organ, each cell plays its role in correcting the problem. Some organs or cells might play a major role, whereas others play a much more minor role. This is of no matter. Each organ or cell has the inherent wisdom to do what is appropriate, what it—as an individual organ or cell—can possibly do in a given situation to solve a given problem impacting the whole body. In health, that is indeed what the human body does.

As members of the body of Christ, we are called to do no less.